Why We Need Dad

WHY WE NEED
DAD

James McQuivey, Ph.D.

PATER
BOOKS

To my Y chromosome and all those who handed it down to me

Contents

Introduction to the Workbook Edition

This isn't the book I expected to make. I had planned to write a book that would cause certain voices in the media to squawk, maybe stimulate some discussion, and be worthy of a dinner conversation or two among people who think about social issues and family trends.

That's not the book I wrote. Because as I compiled the statistics I found that the numbers meant so much more to me when I connected them to my own life experience, to my own father. As you read the book, you'll see that I can hardly bring up a single statistic about fathers without indulging in my own reminiscences about what it was like to be raised by the good man I call Dad.

I wanted everyone else to have the same experience I did of thinking about their fathers throughout the book. But I swiftly recognized a problem of my own making: Releasing *Why We Need Dad* only as an eBook would make it difficult to really engage the words and make them personal for each reader.

That's when I came up with the version you hold in your hands, the workbook edition of *Why We Need Dad*. It has the same text as the original book, but each chapter has had a workbook section added to it designed to give you specific questions you can ask yourself – or others in your family – about your father. I'll ask you to recall and share specific stories or feelings about your dad and even make notes in the workbook so you can make the book a living testament to your father.

There's a fair warning to be offered. The workbook questions are designed for the majority of us – as you'll soon read, the majority of us have dads that were pretty good to us and taught us a lot. But for those of us whose dads were not all that great, especially those of us who truly suffered at the hands of a despot father, the workbook activities may not be a good therapy session because they focus on the average fathers, not the few bad apples out there. My apologies in advance if it proves difficult.

Still, it is my hope that readers of all varieties will find this edition useful. It might even make an excellent family heirloom once it has been marked up and annotated by you and other members of your family. Whatever you do, I hope that reading the book does for you what writing it did for me, namely, that it motivates you to understand and treasure your father.

1: Why I Did This

I remember it in hints and flashes. Throughout that night I regularly leaned forward and lost even more of the contents of my stomach into the big plastic bowl mom had packed for me. The dim fluorescent lights inside the RV would blink on and my father would consider his options: Stay or go?

His decision would have tremendous personal consequences: I desperately did not want to miss the deer hunt, that October school break we rural kids longed for from the moment school started each August. I had begged to go by promising that I would get better. Now, if Dad powered up the rickety RV and drove us home it would mean the end of the hunt for him and my brothers. No hunting, no camping, no eating chocolate licorice around the fire each night.

Decision made, there was a knocking sound followed by a whispered conversation outside the camper of our fellow hunters. Soon the RV motor was running and while I lay deeply fevered we made the several-hour drive back to our small-town hospital emergency room. There the frantic people looking down on me from above – all the world's a ceiling when you're prostrate –

told me not to worry because I didn't even need my appendix. I was in the third grade so I didn't know enough about vestigial organs to object.

Now, nearly 35 years later, I am a father myself, six times over, and I know how impossible a task my own father had that night. When you're a dad, you march to the beat of your own fear that something terrible will befall your child. At its most urgent, that beat sounds the most heart-breaking cadence of all: A warning that the terrible thing that might befall your child is *you* through your own action or inaction, marking the difference between happiness and sadness, or in a worst case, between life and death.

Dad made a good call, delivering me to the right authorities in the nick of time and asking them to remove a vestigial organ for which it has proven true after all these years that I had no need. Ironically, it is of that moment I think when I read in popular media accounts and editorials that men are in a downward spiral. Because to me, the pinnacle of manhood is fatherhood and I cannot imagine removing fathers like some kind of unnecessary organ whose departure might hurt a bit but can easily be overcome.

To be fair, the series of articles I have in mind that have announced the end of men have not argued that men *should* be in decline, only documented that – for many women on the rise, at least – they are. One early dissertation on the decline of men was given to us by Hanna Rosin in the July 2010 pages of *The Atlantic* who politely explained that men can't seem to keep up with women these days. She was preceded in her assessment of men exactly a year before when Sandra Tsing Loh reported in the July 2009 pages of the same publication that, because she committed adultery, marriage must no longer be a useful concept and we should all abandon it. In a similar vein, Kate Bolick last November explained in the same magazine that an attractive and intelligent woman who doesn't want to tie herself down to men – and given the men she describes dating who can blame her – shouldn't have to, leading ultimately to the conclusion that we should all aspire to be like the Mosuo people of southwest China who live in marriage-less households where men are invited into the beds of high-status women at the latter's direction only to be gone by morning.

Bolick seems to suggest that this outcome would be an ideal society for elite females – though I doubt even a majority of elites in our own culture would prefer such an outcome as evidenced by the still-high rates of marriage and childbearing among the top 20% of the population as described recently by Charles Murray in *Coming Apart*, his dour assessment of the unequal distribution of vital family structures. In that much-debated book, Murray describes a number of social traditions that have collapsed in America generally, with the most devastating effect felt in the communities with the fewest economic and social resources where he estimates that 43% to 48% of births in those low-status communities are to unwed mothers. Yet the trend nips at the heels of the top 20 percent: while Murray estimates that only 6% to 8% of their children are born to unwed mothers, the average age at which the married affluent are having children suggests that to them, the opportunity to become parents is one that they delay as long as (and sometimes beyond when) it is biologically possible.

In all of these outcomes, the same culprit is at work: the separation of sex from reproduction. The revolution kicked off by the pill but then spread by every other form of contraceptive – including contraceptive use of abortion – has led to its most logical outcome: men and women both sigh a great relief that they can satisfy their deepest sexual urges and even occasional curiosities without having to ponder their eventual arrival at parenthood.

Some hail this separation while others bemoan it. Regardless of the emotional weight one attaches to it, the facts of this separation can be observed clearly: Fewer people choose to marry, those that do wait until much later to do so. Fewer people choose to have children, and those that do have fewer of them. And some of those that do have children choose to do so without waiting for what prior generations would have considered appropriate circumstances.

It is this last group that is most concerning to some, a group that is, by definition, exclusively female, meaning that women are making decisions about the quality of life of the children they are bringing into the world without fathers to assist them.

Are they doing the right thing? We all know that wonderful woman who, in her late 30s, realized that either due to divorce, slim pickings, or just bad luck, she would not have a husband to help her bring a child into the world and chose not to miss the opportunity to do so. By whatever means, this woman procured a supply of semen and took care of matters on her own. It is my experience that many of these women are remarkable, powerful, and more than adequate mothers.

We also all know that wonderful woman who, in her teens, became pregnant and dropped out of high school to take care of her baby, who battled impossible odds and worked late shifts to raise that child out of poverty by making homework a do-or-die struggle, imparting a new life to her offspring. Though statistically few, I have known these women, too, and I honor them.

But anecdotes aside, is the next generation of children really going to be okay without fathers? What indelible marks, if any, will the absence of a father leave upon their lives?

It's a question that can't be answered with surety looking forward, but some answers can be suggested by looking backward, at the lives of people who have already grown to adulthood with varying types of fathers.

That's why, in December of 2011, I took my own money and commissioned a national survey of 1,000 people ranging in age from 18 to 75 (for more detail on the survey methodology, see Appendix A). Among other things, I survey people for a living, having supervised the survey of over a million people across the years in my career. But this one was different. I wasn't trying to satisfy the conditions of a grant nor was I trying to please a paying client. Because nobody was paying me to do this, the client was myself – and now you – and the objective was simple: Find out if fathers matter and if so, what kinds of fathers matter most.

A note about the Finding Fathers survey:

For those interested in the technical survey details, you can refer to Appendix A at the end of the book. But for the rest of us, I thought it helpful to describe what it means to conduct a national, representative survey of American adults up to age 75 who had fathers. I surveyed a thousand people which is about 600 more than I needed to achieve statistical significance. Because I wanted to divide the respondents into different subgroups, I surveyed more people so I could be accurate in what I say about the subgroups. Some subgroups are bigger than others – so what I say about them is more valid than what I say for smaller groups – but I have chosen not to make statistical analysis a speed bump for the reader and have left it out of the writing. However, rest assured that I applied the same research skills and techniques to this study that I would to any half-million dollar survey funded by a global corporation.

Given the topic, it may puzzle you to find that I only allowed people to participate if they met a specific criterion: they had to have someone in their lives that they considered a father, even if that person did not live in their home or only spent minimal time with them growing up. I did this for a few reasons. It turns out that only 12% of people I sampled claim to have no father figure in their lives. It's such a small group that has very unique demographic characteristics that would undoubtedly provide an exaggerated contrast between people who have fathers and people who don't. Plus, it wouldn't really help us guide the next generation of fathers on what *kind* of fathers they should try to be.

Instead, I chose to survey the spectrum of fathers that raised us. From biological dads who loved their wives to the stepdad that beat his wife and stepchildren. Somewhere across that spectrum, I reasoned, there are some factors that will matter more than others and I wanted to know what they were.

The test is simple: If dads matter, then some kinds of dads should matter more than others, it's just a question of which ones. Of course, it's possible that none of them matter and we can trot merrily off down the path of treating fatherhood like a vestigial appendage.

Workbook 1:

Before we go into the data, answer the following questions about fathers in general. Thinking of all the fathers in America during the years you have been alive, answer the following questions on a scale from 0 to 100 where 100 = 100 out of 100 fathers did this, and 0 = no fathers out of 100 did this.

How many fathers out of a typical 100 spanked their children?

How many fathers out of a typical 100 told their children often that they loved them?

How many fathers out of a typical 100 loved their wives?

How many fathers out of a typical 100 were good providers for their families?

Now ask and answer the same questions about your own father – do so on a scale from 1 to 10 this time, where 1 = not my dad and 10 = completely my dad.

My father spanked me

My father told me often that he loved me

My father loved my mother

My father was a good provider

As a useful exercise, take the numbers in your answers about your own father and add a zero to them. For example, if you put a 7 out of 10 for a particular item, add a zero to the end to make the 7 into a 70. Now compare that number to its counterpart above it. Let's say you estimated that 55 out of 100 typical dads spanked their children. By putting a 7 down (changed to 70) for your own father, you can see that in your mind, your father spanked you more regularly or with more intensity than you assume other people were spanked.

Prior research into these types of beliefs suggests that your estimates of what typical dads do will be influenced by what your own dad did, with a few exceptions. Typically, for reasons that have to do with our sense of threat and security in the world, even if we had a good father who didn't spank us and who told us how often he loved us, we will assume that other people didn't have it as good as we did. In other words, it would not be uncommon for you to rank your dad's love for your mom at an 8 (changed to 80) but then say that 50 out of a typical 100 dads loved their wives.

Our modern media have a tendency to portray the darkest parts of fatherhood and make them seem common even though they are not. I'll save you the academic treatise on why this is not a conspiracy on the part of media professionals in Hollywood and New

York, but the fact is, all of us are hardwired with the same general fear that the world is a scary place. In most of us, it will mean we assume that most fathers are a bit worse than our fathers. For media professionals, it will mean they write books and produce TV shows that do the same. So while it's nobody's fault, it's happening nonetheless and our fathers suffer because of it.

That's one of the reasons I did this research. Tired of reading so much about bad fathers or seeing moronic dads on TV, I wanted to explore just how dark our perceptions of fatherhood are and contrast them with just how good our own fathers were.

To that point, I bet you're interested in the actual facts compared to your estimates. Here are the numbers:

> **35%** of fathers of American adults had fathers that spanked them
>
> **35%** of fathers told their children often that they loved them
>
> **48%** of fathers loved their wives
>
> **72%** of fathers were good providers

Now that you know the facts about fathers, you can start to see how your own father differed from the average father, at least in these few ways. And you can start to see how actual fathers differ from the fathers you assumed were out there.

Did you think more fathers spanked their children than actually did? What was your perception about fathers and their love for their children or their wives? And how did you feel about fathers as good providers?

This is the path I will ask you to go down over and over as you read this book, the path of reflection. Let's take these four points as an example: Ponder each of them – what was your experience like with your father with respect to each of these things? Do you have specific memories associated with these things? How accurate do you think your memories are (check them with siblings if you have them, you'll be amazed at how differently you recall these things)? Take a moment and write some of these thoughts down.

Dad on spanking and discipline:

_____

_____

_____

_____

Dad saying he loved you

_____

_____

_____

_____

Dad loving his wife

_____

_____

_____

_____

Dad as a good provider

_____

_____

_____

_____

With that as a primer, let's dive deeper into why we need dad.

2: What We Got from Dad

James Mackerwithee is my very own Founding Father. Unlike the original men upon whom that title was bestowed, James was not a Revolutionary War hero. He was, in fact, a war loser, a prisoner of war to be exact, most likely captured as a Scottish rebel in either the Battle of Dunbar of 1650 or a subsequent defeat of the Scots in the Battle of Worcester in 1651. And though you don't get statues erected in your honor when you lose a war, I would like to be the first to publicly thank James for losing. Because had he won, I would not be here today. As a prisoner of war, James was brought to the Massachusetts Bay Colony to serve a period of indenture, firmly planting his Scottish feet in American soil, just a few miles from the home where I currently live.

I start with a declaration of my own parentage because by no stretch can you say that I stem from a line of noble men. If I get anything from my fathers, it can't be said that it's privilege, wealth, or prestige. Add up all my McQuiveys from that James to this one and I come from every sort of commoner: a prisoner of war, a widower who built a stone church with his own hands, a shiftless prospector, and most recently a car dealer. And these are just the men from whom I inherit my own copy of the y chromosome, to speak nothing of the infinite number of fathers elsewhere in my family tree.

I am grateful for each one of them and whatever they gave me, whether a spiritual, intellectual, or genetic inheritance, even if by the latter they may have inadvertently left me with poor posture or a faulty heart. Because these fathers of mine gave me the best they could. To honor them best I should aim to do the same. However, this romantic notion of the worth of fathers doesn't really answer the question I have posed: Are dads worth something?

It is certainly true from my own humble experience that dads are great. It wasn't just that night when my appendix met its fateful end, but it was at many different points and in many different ways. From the way my dad taught me to how to love and support a wife by his faithful example. The way he taught me persistence by not letting me quit football or basketball even though I was terrible at both and still am. The way he let me explore the boundaries of courage and stupidity in ways that I did not understand were difficult for him at the time but do now.

Fatherhood has done so much for me, yet I am hesitant to assert that fatherhood is a good thing generally. This is because, effectively conditioned by modern attitudes towards the superfluity or toxicity of dads, I have felt a certain pressure to automatically discount my experience as exceptional. It can't be possible, the former grad student in me whispers, that dads are great, else why would there be so much complaining about them? If patriarchy weren't so pitiful, why would feminism have made the term synonymous with oppression?

I doubt I'm alone in this creeping certainty that to publicly praise the positive power of patriarchy proffers only peril. Lame dads are all around us, at least in the media. Consult the archives of Oprah's Book Club and fathers turn out to be a miserable lot: They beat their children, they abuse their wives, and they sleep around. In literature or movies dads are emotionally unavailable, cold and distant, or just plain absent. Heck, even Disney dads from Cinderella's to the Little Mermaid's are either out of the picture or just – gasp – don't understand their daughters.

But is that really the truth about dads? No. In fact, the short version is that we mostly love our dads and they did right by us. The long version is not much different: We are grateful for our dads and what they did for us and we largely have positive memories of being raised by them – how positive depends on what kind of dad. To illustrate this, I have separated my survey respondents into four groups based on two discriminating variables:

whether they were raised by their biological fathers (in whole or in part) and whether they believe their fathers (biological or not) loved their mothers.

Because this will be so important to the rest of the discussion, let's take some time to consider each of these variables before we crosstabulate them.

Raised by Biological Father

This is the most important variable in the results I will present. I'll give you the answer before I define it so that you know clearly what I'm talking about. A full 64% of respondents indicated that they were raised by their biological father at least in part. They form one group in the survey and I will refer to these people throughout as raised by their biological fathers, biological dads, or biodads for short. The other 36% are referred to as being raised by nonbiological fathers, nonbiological dads, or nonbiodads, if you'll permit me to invent the word for brevity's sake. Here's how I found these people, in my survey I asked this question:

> Q1. Which of the following apply to you (select all that apply):
> 1. I know the identity of my biological father
> 2. I was raised by my biological father (at least in part if not completely)

3.   There is someone (at least one) other than my biological father that I call or consider as a father

4.   I was raised without a father figure of any kind

While 64% of respondents indicated that they were raised by their biological father, an overlapping 22% of people also indicated that there is someone else in their lives beyond their biological fathers that they consider a father. Notice that none of these options are exclusive. In survey speak that means that you could check more than one option and it would make sense. Some combinations are unlikely but possible, such as someone who checked the first three options: yes, I know my biological father's identity; yes, I was raised by him at least in part, and yes, there is someone else I consider a father figure. A small but meaningful 10% of respondents checked all three of those boxes, for example. It is also possible to check boxes one and four, meaning: yes, I know who my father is, but I was raised without a father figure of any kind. These people are the ones that did not qualify for the survey because they couldn't answer questions about the kind of father they had.

For those who indicated they were raised by their biological father at least in part, I also asked the following:

Q2. Were you raised by your biological father

1.   From my birth into adulthood (at least age 18)
2.   From birth until the age _____
3.   Not from birth, but beginning at age: _____

Unlike the above, these answers are exclusive, so you can only answer one of them. Given the complexity of modern fatherhood, I expected that the answers would range widely but they did not most likely because I included people up to the age of 75, people who were raised before the age of no-fault divorce. But even with the rest of us averaged in, a whopping 81% checked the first option while 18% checked the second, with the average age of separation from dad for those people being 12.

Father Loved Mother

This one is a bit trickier especially for the 22% of people who experienced more than one type of father in their lives. To avoid this problem I asked people to choose a father figure that they wanted to answer the survey for, as follows:

Q9. For the purposes of this survey, when we refer to your father, we'd like you to think of the father figure you consider most responsible for making you the person you are today, typically the person who you spent the most time with and had the most opportunity to learn from and observe.

I then asked them to indicate who that person is, with nearly three-fourths choosing to report on their biological father, which is more than were raised by him. It suggests a lot that so many people chose to indicate their biological dad – who did not raise them – as the "father figure you consider most responsible for making you the person you are today."

Now for the love. Later in the survey, when asking questions about the relationship between father and mother – 91% of people indicated they were referring to their biological mother when answering these questions – 48% indicated that father and mother were "very in love." This one is trickier than it seems, however, because for people raised by a divorced mother and father, I had to give them the chance to report on their perception of the love their parents had before the divorce set in. So based on whether people indicated that their parents divorced while they were growing up, they saw one of two different questions:

Option 1 (for people raised by parents that were not divorced while they were growing up):

F12. Through the years you were raised by your father, which of the following things describe the relationship he had with your mother? (select all that apply)

Option 2 (for people raised by parents that were divorced during their growing up years):

F13. Through the years you were raised by your father, prior to the divorce and the events surrounding it that ended their marriage, which of the following things describe the relationship he had with your mother? (select all that apply)

On the list of options to describe the relationship in both cases, one of the items was:

1. My father and mother were very in love

People who checked this box were included in the 48% that were raised in a home where love was present. I will refer to these people as being raised by loving parents, in a home where father loved mother, dad loved mom, or love remained, mostly so it doesn't get repetitive. I will refer to the people outside this group as those raised in homes where father didn't love mother, dad didn't love mom, love was lacking, love was lost, or other semi-poetic terms to represent the loss of something meaningful.

This definition is not perfect for many reasons, not the least of which is that if being raised in a loving home is important, it should be true that the more years you have of this love, the better. But for simplicity's sake, I separate all of us into two camps: you either had love at home or you didn't. It turns out the data support the definition because even through this very simple lens, the role of love comes across as very significant.

Note that this leaves out people who were raised by parents that were not married or were not in couples. These people, by definition, were raised in households where love was less manifest or not even relevant and so these people were automatically categorized as having been raised in homes where father did not love mother. There should be minimal squawking about this from well-meaning people in stable, loving relationships without the bond of marriage. It's true that such couples exist, but they are rare and would not have changed the numbers of the survey in any meaningful way except to bolster the non-loving household group to make them appear less at-risk than they otherwise do.

Identifying How We Were Raised

Cross those two dichotomous variables against each other and you have what consultants lovingly call a two-by-two, a matrix with quadrants representing people who have both of these things (33% of us), people raised by biological father where that love was missing (31%), people who had a nonbiological father that loved their mother (15% of us), and those who had neither a biodad nor a loving nest to come home to (21%) (see figure 1).

Figure 1: The Four Ways We Were Raised

We were raised by either...

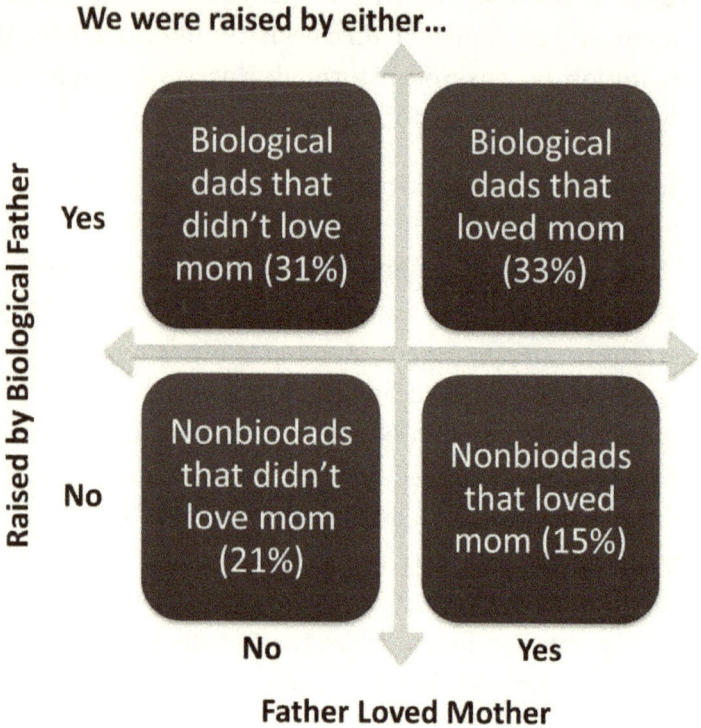

My purpose in combining these two variables is to find out what kind of dad matters most. One that's committed to the family regardless of biological contribution or one that's connected to the family tree by DNA. It doesn't take a rocket scientist – or a social scientist, for that matter – to predict that the best dads, the ones we love the most and did the most for us, are those that are both.

My own dad is both of these things. I took my own survey and my dad scored in the top right quadrant, the "biological father that loved my mother" quadrant. Of course, I didn't need the survey to tell me that, but it was a good validation of the man who let me jump off a 90-foot cliff into the glassy waters of Lake Powell, only to dive in frantically after me when I surfaced with the words, "I can't feel my legs." I didn't need a survey to tell me that such a man would naturally have earned the love and admiration of his sons, especially as they grew to adulthood to find out just how monumental a task he had of raising a family while earning a living – especially maintaining a successful small business in the harrowing Carter years, this latter achievement meriting some kind of medal of honor.

But how do I love my dad? How do you love your dad? Because statistically speaking, it is likely that you do, as my study will show. While we could spend many a Father's Day discoursing on the virtues of our dads, since we have the data let's zero in on the many things our dads did for us. We'll start by determining your own father group. Locate yourself on the matrix I provided. Were you raised by your biological father at least in part? Did your father love your mother "very much" at least in the period before the divorce? It's a judgment call and you are free to alter your definition as you go, but mentally check a box before we proceed. Throughout the chapters that follow, I'll ask you to compare yourself to the responses of other people in your father group to see how your dad stacks up.

This is probably the right time to come back to the 12% of people I sampled who did not qualify for the study because they do not have a father figure of any kind in their lives. I do not have their data so you could claim that they are some kind of exceptional group that will have fared better than the rest of us – free of the burden of patriarchal oppression they have soared higher than most – and I won't have the data to prove you wrong, at least not in my study. But, as you'll see throughout this entire book, there is a clear relationship between what kind of dad you had and how well you – and he – fared. Though I can't prove it, it is safe to assume that the complete lack of any father figure is likely to lead to even less optimal outcomes.

Workbook 2:

Without thinking too hard about it, answer the following questions with your first reaction. Do this on a scale from 1 to 10 where 1 = not at all and 10 = completely.

☐ To your knowledge, how much did your father love your mother/his wife when you were born?

☐ How much did your father love your mother when you were 5?

☐ How much did your father love your mother when you were 10?

☐ How much did your father love your mother when you were 15?

Whether you realize it or not, you have just created a chart tracking the love you believe your father had for your mother across the first fifteen years of your life. What's the shape of that curve? Does it start high and stay high or does it see-saw up and down? Based on my memories and what I know about my parents' lives together I would guess that their numbers started better than average (say a 6 or a 7) and rose slowly over those years. But I can't really say for sure that there weren't dips and valleys along the way.

What about your parents? Chances are good that if you're reading this book it's because you had a better-than-average father situation – that's just the nature of someone who would read a book about why we need dads – but that still doesn't mean your parents had the perfect marriage, so many of your lines may start high and dip low. Many will end altogether, either in divorce or in what we commonly call a loveless marriage.

Of course, you don't know the real answers to these questions, you only have *your perceptions*. To get a bigger view, share this quiz with your siblings without letting them see your answers. Then compare their answers to yours. You'll notice some differences. Disclose and discuss the differences. That will be a good time to go to the next questions and challenge yourself to recall either memories or family stories that help you determine how much love your father had for your mother at different points. You can do this exercise alone or with your siblings and see what different memories they come up with. I've left you some room to jot notes down from the conversation you have together.

Stories or memories about dad loving mom when you were born

_____

_____

_____

_____

Stories or memories about dad loving mom when you were 5-years old

_____

_____

_____

_____

Stories or memories about dad loving mom when you were 10-years old

_____

_____

_____

_____

Stories or memories about dad loving mom when you were 15-years old

_____

_____

_____

_____

Other memories about mom and dad's relationship?

_____

_____

_____

_____

The final challenge: If you are up to it, share this section – all these memories and your perceptions – with your father if he's still alive. Sit him down for Father's Day or any day and ask him to tell you about his love for your mother. Share your memories with him and tell him what his love for your mother taught you about love.

A note on this one. A lot of us are hesitant to discuss these emotional issues with our fathers, especially if things were rocky at times in the home. You're the best judge of whether this is too much to ask your father to discuss openly, but if you feel the time is right, I encourage it. Even if your parents' relationship wasn't always perfect – even if it ended in divorce – it's important that a father let his children know that their parents did love each other.

Finally, an invitation: If these or other memories brought to mind by this book have been meaningful to recall and you are willing to share, I encourage you to go to facebook.com/WhyWeNeedDad and post a memory or two.

3: Dad Was a Man of Character

Though I'm not old enough to have caught the series in its original run, *The Andy Griffith Show* was, in 1967, the most popular show on television, when nearly 30% of US households watched it in a typical week. The show often centered on the doings of Andy's son Opie and his continual tendency to learn life lessons by making modest mistakes. A typical episode ended with Andy having to explain proper behavior to Opie and asking him to do the right thing – either to apologize to the grocer or stand up to the new bully in town. In these shows, Andy was a man of integrity, full of life lessons.

To our modern sensibilities, Andy Griffith is a fraud, the way that TV's Mr. Brady was eventually exposed as a fraud – an oft-intoxicated actor pretending to dispense paternal wisdom in order to make a buck. We are told routinely to look at the naïve portrayals of such TV fathers on *Father Knows Best* or *Leave It To Beaver* and doubt their veracity. Surely men in that era weren't that good, were they? And already knowing the answer to our own question we explain this tremendous interest in the small-town values of a humble sheriff and his son as an outlier. Either people didn't have much else to watch or they indulged in these simple fantasies because they were escapist fun.

But consider, as I instructed my survey respondents to do, the following list of adjectives with respect to your own father. Was he: strong, intelligent, responsible, loving, kind, and courageous or was he intimidating, angry, mean, abusive, and disappointed? These are just a handful of adjectives I asked people to indicate if they applied to their fathers while they were being raised by them. And, not coincidentally, they are listed above in

Figure 2: The Attributes That Describe Our Fathers

Thinking about your father's general character over the time he was raising or helping raise you, please indicate how much you think the following attributes described him during that time.

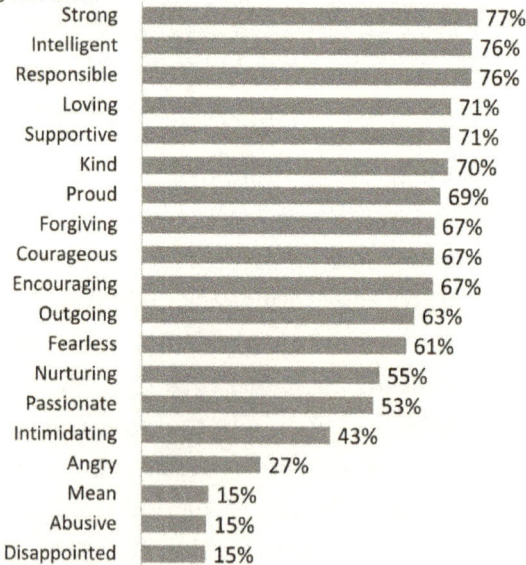

Attribute	Percent
Strong	77%
Intelligent	76%
Responsible	76%
Loving	71%
Supportive	71%
Kind	70%
Proud	69%
Forgiving	67%
Courageous	67%
Encouraging	67%
Outgoing	63%
Fearless	61%
Nurturing	55%
Passionate	53%
Intimidating	43%
Angry	27%
Mean	15%
Abusive	15%
Disappointed	15%

Percent that check the top 2 boxes on a 5-point scale; Base: all respondents, n=1000 the exact descending order in which they were indicated by my respondents. A full 77% of us believe our fathers were strong, falling down bit by bit until we get to the 67% of us that think our fathers were courageous (see figure 2).

Before you go on, review the list yourself. You can answer this for your own father in one of two ways. You can either check each attribute that applies to your father, or you can imagine a scale from 1 to 10 where a 1 means does not describe my father and 10 means describes my father completely. If you choose to go with the 10-point scale, it gives you a handy way to compare your answers to the average. If, for example, you checked a 7 or 8 out of 10 to describe your father as strong, your answer comes in roughly at the same strength of the average father (77%). You can employ this 1 to 10 trick throughout these chapters to get a similar comparison.

All the positive adjectives I listed were checked by a majority of respondents, regardless of their own father status. In fact, the respondents with the least going for them in their family history – those raised by nonbiological fathers that did not love mother – scored their fathers slightly higher on every positive dimension.

As for the negative adjectives, 43% of us think our fathers were intimidating – not necessarily a negative but the highest-scoring of the negative items on the list.

This was also independent of our father status. From there, the agreement drops precipitously – 27% think dad was angry, while 15% think dad was mean, abusive, or disappointed.

In survey research, you should know your topic well enough to anticipate the likely answers to your questions. This requires background research and preparation, examination of prior studies and available literature and other things that most people don't care about. But I'll admit I didn't expect the answers I got to this question. First, I couldn't find anyone who had asked questions like this, but I also thought I understood the range of emotions that people have towards their fathers. After all, I had seen *Dead Poets Society*. So I didn't think getting a mix of positive and negative responses on this list of adjectives would be that challenging.

Yet, across the board, even those of us who we'll later learn are not happy with the way dad managed things, preferred to use only positive adjectives to describe our dads. Still, this isn't what we see in the discussion about and portrayals of fathers in the world around us. Ironically, it was Opie's next successful show – *Happy Days* – that casually introduced to us the loveable but ineffectual father, Mr. Cunningham, played by a well-meaning Tom Bosley who later traded in his father credentials to pitch that most fatherly of household accessories: two-ply garbage bags.

Trace a line more or less straight from *Happy Days* through *Rosanne*, on to *The Simpsons* and finally to *Modern Family*, certainly the most sophisticated of these efforts to portray dads in what is not always a negative light, but a very dim one. One in which they rarely, if ever, rise to demonstrate the genuine strength, intelligence, responsibility, love, kindness, and courage that Andy Griffith did, the same attributes we overwhelmingly attribute to our own fathers.

It is attributes like these that make us want to be like our fathers. Even when we initially resist it. When I was in grade school, our family would occasionally go for Sunday walks in the empty fields behind our house. My parents would hold hands and stroll leisurely down the dirt roads that threaded through the various fields, occasionally my father had to hold some barbed wire open for my mother to climb through, and we boys would throw rocks at fence posts or chase down a huge flying grasshopper against which we bore some kind of primal malice.

Growing up in the high desert of Utah, water was a carefully controlled resource and it didn't flow freely over or through these fields, rather it was carefully guided through networks of irrigation ditches that ran at seemingly irregular intervals. This meant that everywhere you looked the ground was dry and the weeds grew brown. But lining each field would be a ditch that permitted actual green growth. Though farmers routinely burned these ditches to keep the weeds from slowing the water's course (or worse, drinking it all up along the way), in between scorchings you could find a thriving culture of weeds, grasshoppers, toads, and occasionally, wild asparagus.

For those of you who didn't know that asparagus grows wild in irrigation ditches in Utah, welcome to my world. Better said, welcome to my dad's world. Invariably on our periodic walks through the fields my father and mother would slow down as they approached a ditch, they would incline a few degrees to peer into the ditch beside them, and would proclaim, "There's one!"

This would be stated in a tone that resembled a declaration of victory. This was a bizarre thing for me then because the idea of being glad you found wild asparagus among the weeds *in the dirt* was about as satisfying as finding spoiled milk pooled on the floor of the carport. When asparagus of any variety fails to move you, as it did to me then, the idea of finding it in a ditch where your friends often relieved themselves on the long walk home from school, was anything but a thrill.

"We're going to wash it when we get home," my father would say as if that justified it, bundling up the scraggly things in his arms and carrying his precious cargo with face all smiles.

The word asparagus actually connects to my dad in my brain. I cannot think of the former without immediately conjuring the latter. But it was not merely his habit of finding random asparagi in the ditches of my childhood, it was the way he giddily defended his practice from our escalating ridicule. He always resorted to two techniques that were unassailable, despite our youthful confidence. First, he would offer the obvious yet hard-to-refute rebuttal: You don't know if you like it until you try it. Guilty as charged.

Second, he did something that was so smart, so infinitely wise and manipulative that I have copied it a thousand times over. He would say, "Good! You boys don't want any, that means more for me!" And darn it if he didn't mean it.

Brilliant. This many decades later, I absolutely love asparagus. I don't know how to describe this attribute of a father in so few words so I didn't ask people in my survey whether their dads manipulated them into loving healthy vegetables, but I doubt I'm the only one that became the very person he thought he was mocking.

* * *

It is hard to say what motivated me to try out for the middle school basketball league. It certainly wasn't because I wanted to give my father the chance to teach me what it means to be a man of integrity. Instead, it was probably just that my friends were going down to the tryouts, I was bored, and I was getting even taller, putting me and others at risk of the mistaken assumption that being tall equals being a good basketball player.

Tryouts consisted of shooting baskets at the gym in the old armory – free-throw shots, layups, anything that would showcase your general ability, or inability as the case may be. I played so terribly that I was sure I wouldn't get picked up by any of the teams.

Except that I did. Like some kind of official draft process, each team had a specific slot in the lineup and used its points to pick the kids they hoped would fill the holes in their team. I got picked up by a scrappy little team that had some great guards, a couple of power forwards, but happened to lack a tall guy in the middle. Oops. I was now part of a team.

Long story short, I hated practice. Did you know they expect you to run up and down the court, over and over, until you want to puke and they call that *training*? And I was lousy in our games – they were nothing like the inspirational sports movies I had spent more hours watching than actually playing the sport. That's why after just a few weeks of this special form of torture I made up my mind: I was going to quit.

Enter my father. I don't remember how I told him I was going to quit nor how much time elapsed between the decision I made and the conversation that ensued, but suffice it to say that Dad made it very clear that I could not quit. There was no shaming about how he wouldn't let his son grow up to be a quitter, that was not Dad's style. Instead, he painted the situation in very clear terms: The team had used up its one slot to recruit a center on me. If I quit, the coach would have no way to fill that void. Therefore, by quitting, I was failing to honor an agreement I had voluntarily made that would harm someone to whom I had made a promise. If I backed out I would be failing to live up to my commitment.

And that, I later realized he was saying though he didn't put it into words that night, was something we McQuiveys just don't do.

Workbook 3:

Quick, without thinking too hard, what TV show dad reminds you most of your own father?

_____

Without meaning any disrespect to your own father, what TV show dad(s) do you wish you could have been raised by, even for just a short while? Why?

_____

_____

_____

This is another good one to ask your siblings to answer. Especially if they were far enough away from you in years so that they grew up watching different TV shows than you did.

Now I'll give you the space to do the exercise I proposed in the chapter. For each of the following attributes, rate whether the attribute describes your father on a scale from 1 to 10 where 1 = does not describe my father and 10 = describes my father completely.

     ___ Strong
     ___ Intelligent
     ___ Responsible
     ___ Loving

__ Supportive
__ Kind
__ Proud
__ Forgiving
__ Courageous
__ Encouraging
__ Outgoing
__ Fearless
__ Nurturing
__ Passionate
__ Intimidating
__ Angry
__ Mean
__ Abusive
__ Disappointed

The actual responses in the chapter are on page 34 so you can go back and compare your dad point for point to the average dad in the population.

How does your dad fare? Are there any surprises in the comparison to the typical dad? Were there some attributes that were just hard to answer? For me, it was hard to describe my father as courageous as long as I defined courageous as stopping bullets or fighting off lions. Of course, that's not what courageous has to mean. And the fact that two-thirds of us think our dads are courageous suggests that either a lot of bullets are being stopped in their tracks or that most people are looking for courage in other things. Where in your father's life do you see courage?

Pick a few attributes either from this list or others that you think are especially apt descriptors of your father. Then add some thoughts about why you rated your father the way you did. What memories or experiences led you to feel the way you do about him? Then, if he's still living, share some of these memories with him.

Attribute: _____

_____

_____

_____

_____

Attribute: _____

_____

_____

_____

_____

4: Dad Was a Hard Worker

Maybe now that women outnumber men in most college majors it's okay to talk openly about the idea that many men achieve a great satisfaction from providing for their families without people assuming that you're trying to keep women down. Despite whatever rumors you have heard in the past about how this patriarchal pattern is oppressive, it turns out that the vast majority of us were raised by a dad who was either the sole (42%) or primary provider (44%). Certainly this is one fact that has been trending down, but even among the younger half of my respondents, those under 40, 34% of them were raised by a sole provider dad. And dads that don't provide at all are rare – only 5% of people with a father had one that did not have any role as a provider. I know that raising these numbers will cause a reflexive anger in some who believe that giving dad the provider role is a bad thing, a leftover remnant from a past in which men ruled over their families by controlling the family finances. And certainly there are outlier families in which such inappropriate fathering occurred. Yet from the perspective of those of us who grew up in these dads' homes, it appears that this patriarchy didn't harm most of us at all.

Eighty-two percent of us whose fathers provided at all believe our fathers were "hard workers." Those of us with biodads that loved our moms put this number at 94% compared to the 65% of those at the opposite end of the matrix (see figure 3).

Figure 3: Most Dads Worked Hard

Agree with the statement, "My father was a hard worker"

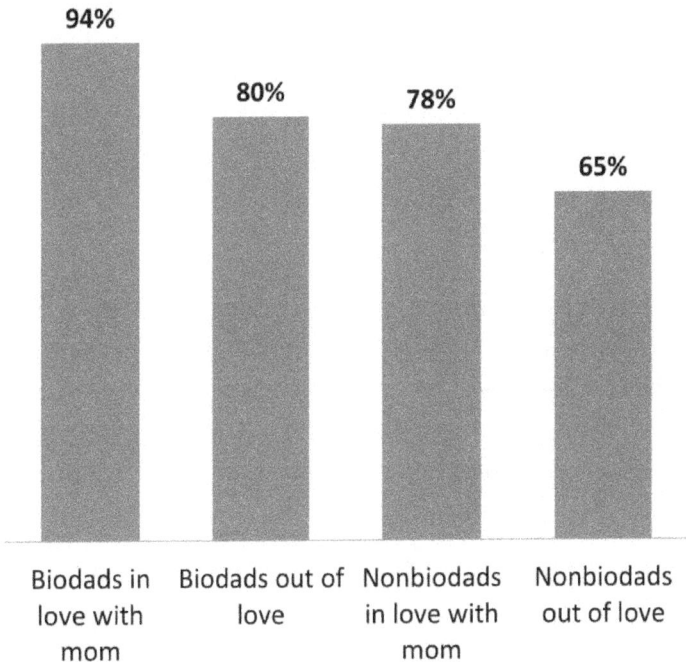

Base: Those whose fathers were providers at any level; n=952

Though there is a significant difference between the two numbers, note that even at the low end, nearly two thirds of those with the least advantaged father situations ascribe the virtue of hard work to our fathers. And being a hard worker correlates with our feelings about whether dad was a "good provider," which should come as a relief to hard-working dads everywhere. The one interesting difference here is the middle groups – those with biodads that didn't love mom and those with nonbiodads that did. Where they were in a statistical dead heat on the question of whether dad was a hard worker, coming in at 80% and 78% respectively, in the case of whether dad was a good provider, they diverge. Here, 87% of us with nonbiodads that loved mom think he was a good provider compared to 68% of those with a biodad that didn't love mom.

Hardly evidence of a causal relationship, it is worth asking the question: Does a dad who loves mom work harder for her? My own experience suggests that is the case but because I'm a statistician I won't claim that my own desire to please my wife by bringing home the fruits of my labors so she can enjoy them is anything more than my experience. But the depth to which I feel that joy is impossible to dismiss, even if certain academics or journalists would choose to imagine me as a caveman, dragging my "kill" home in hopes that it will warm my wife's heartfires.

In fact, most of us think that providing for a family ranks at the top of a list of six things dads can do for their families. I gave people a list of six roles that a father can play: provide for his family, protect his family, nurture his children, prepare his children for the future, teach his children, and discipline his children. I did not give them in that order but that is the order that people ranked them in importance for fathers, with "provides for his family" coming in a clear lead for all four segments (see figure 4).

Figure 4: Providing Ranks at the Top of Six Roles of a Father

Ranked by respondents in priority from top to bottom.

A good father...
1. Provides for his family
2. Protects his family
3. Nurtures his children
4. Prepares his children for the future
5. Teaches his children
6. Disciplines his children

Base: All respondents; n=1000

Note that I did not ask them if this function should be fulfilled to the exclusion of mom's ability or desire to earn an income as well. I avoided creating this false dilemma in the survey for precisely the same reason I think we as a society should avoid it: it's okay to acknowledge that men – especially good, loving men, the kind we are grateful raised us and the kind we probably want to raise the next generation – not only derive great satisfaction from providing for their families, but they make their families proudest of them when they do so. Whether or not mom is also a breadwinner.

With all this providing going on, it should not surprise us, then, that of the values we believe we learned from our dads – and they are many – the top-ranked lesson is "the importance of hard work," which 74% of us thank our fathers for instilling in us. Here again the distribution of responses see-saws on its way down: 86% of the top quadrant thanks dad for this, 69% for those with biodads that did not love mom, followed at 75% by those with nonbiodads who loved mom, and 59% of those with nonbiodads who did not love mom (see figure 5). Even though the downward trend is again present, still a majority of even the least advantaged group agrees that dad taught the value of hard work.

In the ill-fated hunting trip that ended in my appendectomy, one of the families we were traveling with happened to be that of one of my father's most long-tenured car salesmen. Growing up in a small town where I regularly rode my bike to what we called downtown – the little strip of businesses that included my father's car dealership – I had ample time to watch my father interact with the people that worked for him. I

Figure 5: Most Fathers Taught the Value of Hard Work

Percent that feel like they learned "the importance of hard work" from their father

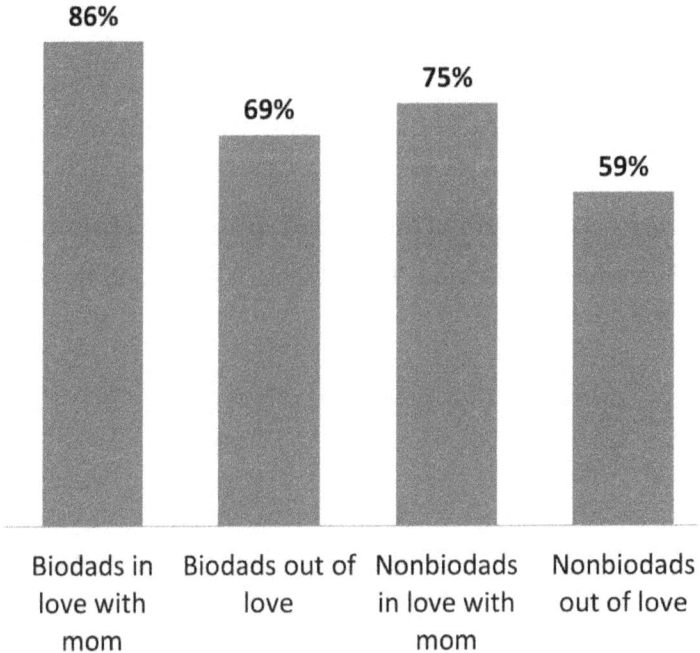

Biodads in love with mom	Biodads out of love	Nonbiodads in love with mom	Nonbiodads out of love
86%	69%	75%	59%

Base: All respondents; n=1000

did not think of them as his employees because he did not act as though they were his subordinates. I was received warmly by them with only a few exceptions – and those typically because I was acting out the role of the dealer's brat, a universal title known around the car dealerships of that era to describe the owner's kids. I was given this otherwise warm treatment, I understand now, because of who he was.

Given how much my own father was respected by the people he worked with, I thought to include this statement in the survey: "My father was respected by his peers at work." A full 84% of us with biodads that loved mom agree with this statement (see figure 6). Here is another place where the middle groups diverge in interesting ways. Of those of us with biodads who didn't love mom, 56% report that dad was respected at work,

Figure 6: Dad Earned the Respect of His Colleagues

Percent that indicated "My father was respected by his peers at work"

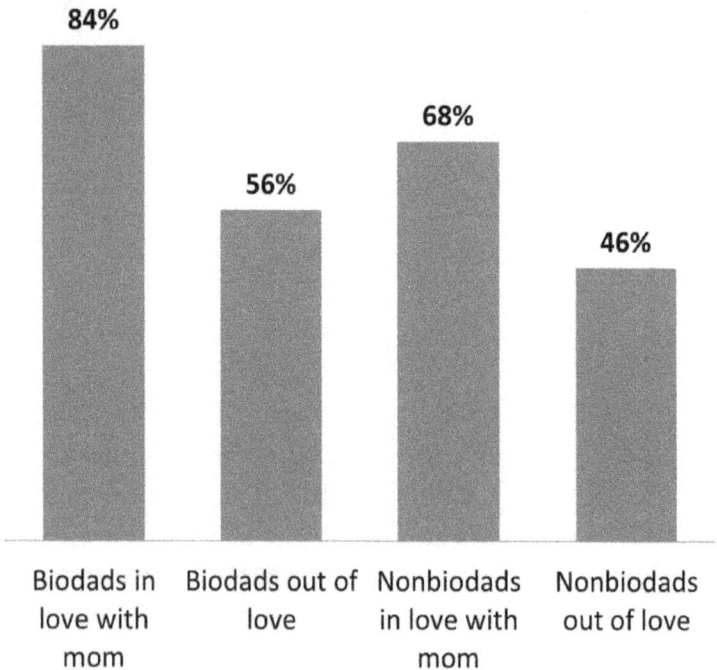

Base: Those whose fathers were providers at any level; n=952

compared to the 68% of nonbiodads who loved mom. Coming in at 46% are the members of the bottom quadrant, those raised by nonbiodads who didn't love mom. As a separate note, I am not sure what to make of this fact: Regardless of who raised us, if we are under 40, just 59% of us think our fathers were respected at work compared to the 73% of people 40 and up who think that about their dads. Is it possible that the de-emphasis of the role of fathers as providers has reduced the opportunity for us to learn about our fathers' performance at work?

One potential negative outcome of all this work is the workaholic dad – the one we often see in movies about broken family life in busy cities like New York. This is a real problem, certainly, and 24% of us agree that "my father was busy with work or other things and didn't take much time with me." The numbers aren't high, but any number is distressing. What's most distressing, however, is where the numbers sit. The winner, if you can call it that, is the biodad who didn't love mom. An eye-opening 39% of his children agree with this statement, followed by the children of nonbiodads who didn't love mom, who came in at 23% (see figure 7). If there was love in the home, the tendency to use work as an escape route reduced markedly, coming in at 18% of biodads who loved mom and just 10% of nonbiodads who loved mom.

Figure 7: Lover Dads Are Less Likely to Be Workaholics

"My father was busy with work or other things and didn't take much time with me."

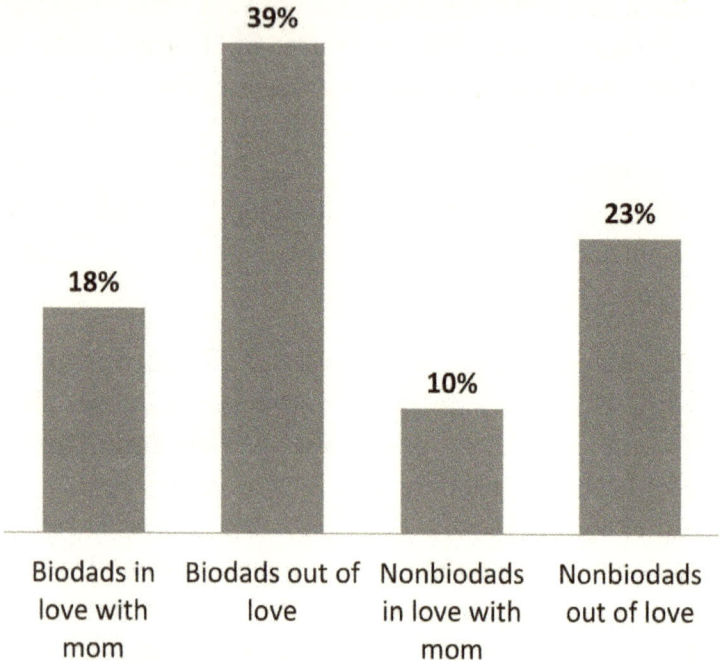

18%	39%	10%	23%
Biodads in love with mom	Biodads out of love	Nonbiodads in love with mom	Nonbiodads out of love

Base: All respondents; n=1000

Given the prevalence of these work-distracted dads in film and TV portrayals, it is fair to ask whose dads these writers and producers are portraying: if not ours, then perhaps theirs?

Not coincidentally, the second thing on the list of fatherly priorities all of my survey respondents agreed upon is closely related. If dad is first a provider, he is next a protector. Just a few years ago I witnessed an unexpected crossing of those two roles in my own experience.

For a profession I keep an eye on new technology. I'm currently helping people in the media business – TV makers, book publishers, cable companies – figure out how to deal with the Kinect for Xbox 360, the Kindle Fire, and everything else about to come. When I fly, which is often, I use my flight time to scan for statistically irrelevant anecdotes to shape my research. Some years ago, when the Video iPod was new, I wanted to see whether people would watch movies on the novel but tiny screen.

I remember the first time I saw a man next to me pull out a Video iPod on a plane. It was a cross-country flight to Seattle, plenty of time to watch a movie, I figured, so I waited and spied. For much of the flight he listened to music, but at one point, he thumbed through some photos of his family. And then, like magic, he did it, he pulled up a video. Only it wasn't a blockbuster movie or an independent film. It was a home movie of himself skiing with his children. Chalk one up for fatherhood.

This came full-circle many plane-based spy sessions later, when I found myself sitting next to a man with a much more sophisticated portable device, a phone this time – the passage of time does amazing things for technology – and watched him thumb through a whole host of movies he had stored for later retrieval. Sometime later, out of the corner of my eye I recognized a scene in the movie he had chosen, a scene in which a mission-driven Liam Neeson tortures an Albanian Kidnapper to both determine the whereabouts of his stolen daughter and exact a tidy revenge on the evil man.

I couldn't take my eyes off it from that moment forward. I really should have minded my own business, but as scene after scene unfolded – in a movie, *Taken*, that I had already seen three times – I eagerly followed vengeful dad Liam on his purposeful, bloody path to retrieve his daughter.

There are many disclaimers I should add about this movie: It's violent, it's probably unfair to Albanian people, and it's downright mean. I'm the guy that believes in things like turn the other cheek and all that. But every time I watch this movie, I recite the lines with Liam when he says to the kidnappers on the phone at the end of act one: "I will look for you, I will find you and I will kill you."

When we landed I introduced myself to my seat mate and mentioned that I hoped he didn't mind that I couldn't take my eyes off the movie he was watching ("for a few minutes" I said, compressing the truth a little).

"Was that the first time you've seen that movie?" I asked.

"No, I've seen it a dozen times, I own it, I watch it all the time."

"Can I ask?" I started hesitantly, "Do you have any daughters?"

His voice fairly boomed as he answered. "Yes, two of them, one in her twenties and one in her teens."

"I have a 17-year old," I told him. And in that moment we bonded in a way that men only do around things like war, football, and exterminating the men that kidnap their daughters.

When considering fathers in film and popular culture, Neeson's character may not exactly be Atticus Finch from *To Kill a Mockingbird*, but he is, despite his brutality, among the most sympathetic. At least to men who have daughters.

Workbook 4:

Answer these questions on a scale from 1 to 10 where 1 = does not describe my father and 10 = describes my father completely:

☐ My father was a hard worker

☐ I learned the value of hard work from my father

☐ My father was respected by his peers at work

☐ My father was busy with work and didn't take much time with me

One thing I didn't mention in the book is that in the survey I asked each of the 1,000 respondents to indicate in a fill-in-the-blank way what kind of work their fathers did – at least for the majority of their careers. I was astonished at the range of responses from people but also pleased that people not only wanted to fill in the blank but sometimes added more detail to the job description than I asked for. This insistence on detail made me wonder to what extent people's identities of their families growing up were tied up with the kind of work their fathers did.

You already know my father was a car dealer. This is something I am both immensely proud of but also have to defend a bit – let's just say that dishonesty is an occupational hazard in that profession and I saw my father work hard to be an honest small-town car dealer. I'll save those stories for my next book, perhaps, but now it's your turn to conjure up your own stories. By this time you know I will encourage you to share these stories with your siblings and your parents as you feel appropriate.

How did your father's profession define your sense of family as you were growing up?

_____

_____

_____

_____

What memories do you have that taught you the value of hard work?

_____

_____

_____

_____

I also asked people whether or not they learned the value of a dollar from their fathers – 66% said yes. But, interestingly, just 42% of us say we learned that a "penny saved is a penny earned" from dad. There's a lot to explore here, especially as it relates to what kind of profession your dad worked in. If he made more money than others, did it make you value money more or take it more for granted?

Were you aware of your relative wealth or poverty growing up? Take some time and reflect on whether you have any deep feelings or memories about what it was like to grow up with the economic resources you did or did not have. Did you have to wear hand-me-down jeans with patches in the knees or were you the kid with the newest Garanimals at the beginning of the school year? Have you ever asked your father how he felt about being a provider? Do you think it provided a sense of satisfaction to him, was it deeply stressful, or was it just part of a day's work for him? You know what's next:

_____

_____

_____

_____

_____

5: Dad Showed Us How to Make Marriage Work

The decision to have a child is not an easy one. It wasn't for me and I'm a Mormon, people known for embracing marriage and parenthood, multiple times over (the parenthood, that is, the marriage thing we only do once, at least at a time, despite what you've seen on HBO).

Ask men who are fathers, as I did in my study, what the effect of parenthood on the marriage is and 74% will tell you to "make sure your marriage is strong as possible before having children." Though almost as many – 64% – will add that "your wife will love you more if you are a good father," so at least the right incentives are in place.

Not that I didn't want to be a father, I did, from a very early age. It's that I had no idea how to be one. I'm the youngest of three children and none of my siblings preceded me in marriage or in parenthood. Even my closest cousins were either younger than me or slower to the marriage thing so I had scant immediate examples to look to while growing up.

Let's be clear on what this means: I didn't know how to change a diaper, I didn't know how to feed a baby, I didn't know how to schedule a playdate. These are just a few of a thousand things I didn't know how to do before I became a father.

Plus there was the whole neo-feminist thing that I had to deal with. I blame my mother: I read all of her women's magazines growing up. Read enough women's magazines over enough time and you're bound to be left with your head spinning. By the time I was ready to marry I had some pretty conflicting ideas about what a woman really wants (or should want) from life generally or from a husband specifically.

That's why, as a young husband I sat my wife down to have the talk. We were both finishing college and making career plans. I thought I'd do us both a favor and just put the topic on the table

"Sweetheart," I started, "I want you to know that I don't want you to feel pressured to give up your career just to have children."

She answered with a bewildered "Huh?" or something to that effect.

"I just want you to know that the decision of when to have children and how to manage that responsibility is really yours and you can take as much time as you want. If you want to wait and have children later after your career is more established, we can do that."

"Huh?" She probably didn't say this again, but it was clearly what she was thinking.

I paused and waited for the immense grandness of what I was saying to sink in. Within minutes I expected she would thank me for being so considerate and open-minded and that we'd have some kind of sensitive, modern relationship from that point on. I was wrong.

"What's the point of that?" She finally managed.

"Huh?" Now it was my turn.

"What's the point of getting married then?"

"Huh?" Again.

"I mean, isn't that the whole point? Didn't we get married so we could have children and be a family?"

If I remember right, she was starting to get upset with me. As if I was trying to back out of the whole deal she clearly thought we had made when we looked at each other across the altar of marriage.

"Yeah, well, yeah, that is kind of the whole point."

I did not get the Joe Sensitive pat on the back I expected. And now, two decades later, I'm very glad I didn't because she was right and I was wrong. We were parents just over a year later and the resulting years of parenting together have forged a tight link between the two of us that I am committed to ensuring never breaks.

I went through a phase in fifth grade where I decided that my parents weren't affectionate enough in front of us kids. It's not that they weren't affectionate at all, but I had developed the notion, most likely from watching TV, that a husband and wife should engage in a ritual greeting and kiss each day when they separated in the morning and were rejoined in the evening.

I'm sure they felt a bit judged by their son, but my parents obliged my request that each morning they kiss and say something to the effect of, "Goodbye, sweetheart." My parents were never ones to indulge in pet names in front of us, but when I asked them to come up with an appropriate appellation, I believe my parents revealed that "honeybun" was the *nom d'amour* my father employed for my mother.

I dutifully inspected their daily routine to ensure that they complied with my invented sign of devotion. It speaks volumes that they were willing to go through with it to show their youngest – and clearly spoiled – son that they did, in fact, love each other.

Teaching sons and daughters how a man should love a woman is one of the most important things I believe fathers do. And I shudder to think of how boys raised without fathers that love their wives – or without fathers at all – will ever learn this. On one occasion my father-in-law Brian was working with a group of younger men in their early twenties and he made a passing affectionate reference to my mother-in-law. One of these men took out a notebook and scribbled something down. When asked, he confessed that he was writing down examples of how Brian spoke to and about his wife. He explained that in his home his father had been long absent so he had never seen how a married relationship should function. Until he worked with my in-laws it had not occurred to him that a husband can and probably should speak respectfully, admiringly, and lovingly about his spouse in and out of her presence.

That's the power of fathers when it is achieved but it also highlights the weakness of fathers when they abdicate their fatherly responsibility. Gratefully, 60% of us whose parents stayed married during our youth believe that "father and mother were very in love." Sadly but not unexpectedly, only 22% of us whose parents split before we reached adulthood or were never married in the first place are willing to say the same about our parents' relationship even prior to the divorce.

The list of positive outcomes that correlate with that love is long and obvious, including, "my father supported my mother," "father thought mother was beautiful," and "father treated my mother with respect," all of which range from a high of 54% to a low of 46% for all of us, whether our parents stayed married or not. This is where my segmentation of fathers really shines through, of course, such that if we were raised by biological fathers that loved our mothers, 77% of us agree that dad

Figure 8: When Dad Loves Mom, Everything is Better

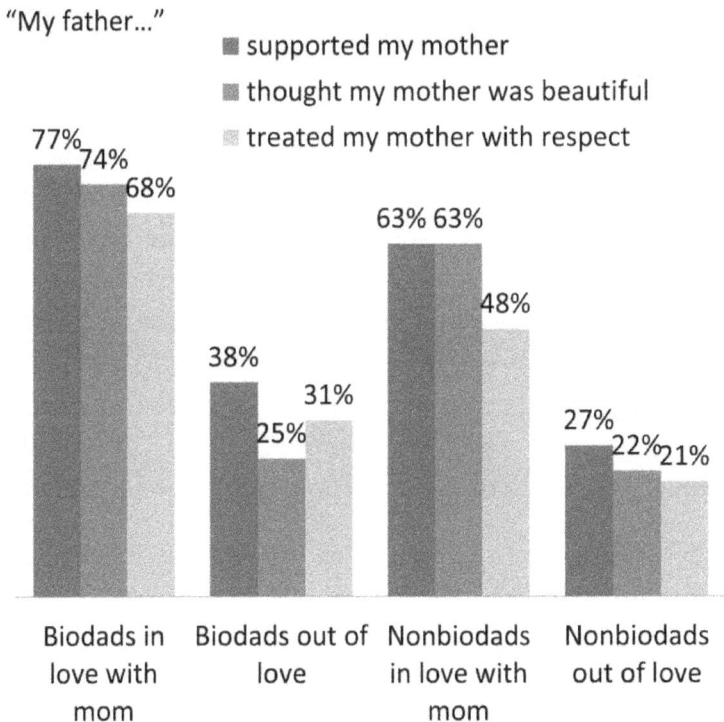

"My father…"
- supported my mother
- thought my mother was beautiful
- treated my mother with respect

Biodads in love with mom: 77%, 74%, 68%
Biodads out of love: 38%, 25%, 31%
Nonbiodads in love with mom: 63%, 63%, 48%
Nonbiodads out of love: 27%, 22%, 21%

Base: Those raised by married parents at least for some period; n=919
For divorced parents, respondents replied for the pre-divorce period

supported mom, 74% say he thought she was beautiful, and 68% think he treated her with respect (see figure 8).

Sadly, even in homes where nonbiodads loved mom, the numbers, while positive, do not reach the same heights, coming in at a disappointing 63%, 63%, and 48%, respectively. Generally in my survey, nonbiodads fare pretty well as long as they loved mom; however, this is one instance in which it's clear that there's something unique about being raised by a biological father. But what is it, really? My survey can't answer that, but the possible answers are intriguing. It would not be hard to imagine that men who raise their own offspring have a more significant level of commitment to the family and thus the marriage. This could be psychological or it could even be hormonal in nature. Or it could also be that children raised by biological dads perceive them to be more in love and more committed regardless of their actual behavior, again for reasons not available to conscious scrutiny. Either way, the data are unambiguous that this is one area where biodads lead.

It is worth a pause here to address a thorny issue. So far I have recited data with occasional personal notes about what it's like to come from an advantaged family situation. I hope these data and even my anecdotes are helpful for most. But for those who are stepdads, I realize that it can also come as a slap in the face. Here you are, doing your best, and along I come, throwing these data at you to prove that you face unbeatable odds. In a worst-case scenario, this information could lead you to throw up your arms in despair and detach from your spouse and your family. Of course, were you to do that, you would be proving that your category defines you. I encourage you to pursue the best-case scenario. Prove that you can climb that hill, even if it is a little steeper. The good news is, though the hill is indeed a bit steeper, on average, for men in your situation, it's not impossible to scale and as I've already shown, you have plenty of opportunities to earn the respect, admiration, and love of your step-children.

Also, I am happy to report that few of our fathers really blew it in the category of showing love by showing its opposite. Just 17% of us whose parents stayed together report that our parents fought often. And even for those whose parents did divorce before adulthood, only a minority – 37% – say that their parents fought each other often. And here's the most powerful evidence to counter years of reading Oprah's Book Club: In in-tact families, only 5% of us say that father was "physically abusive to my mother," which compares to a sad but thankfully low 19% among those that divorced before my survey respondents reached adulthood.

And, all these years later, I can be relieved to find out that my concerns about my parents' physical affection in front of us – at least defined by me in the fifth grade as a morning kiss and affectionate greeting – was not uncommon, even among happy marriages. Not that I should have been worried since they have now been married a grand total of 50 years. But in this respect, they were not alone. Only 30% of all of us say that our parents were physically affectionate in front of us, a number that rises to 48% if we were raised by biodads

Figure 9: Dad and Mom Had More Going On Than We Saw

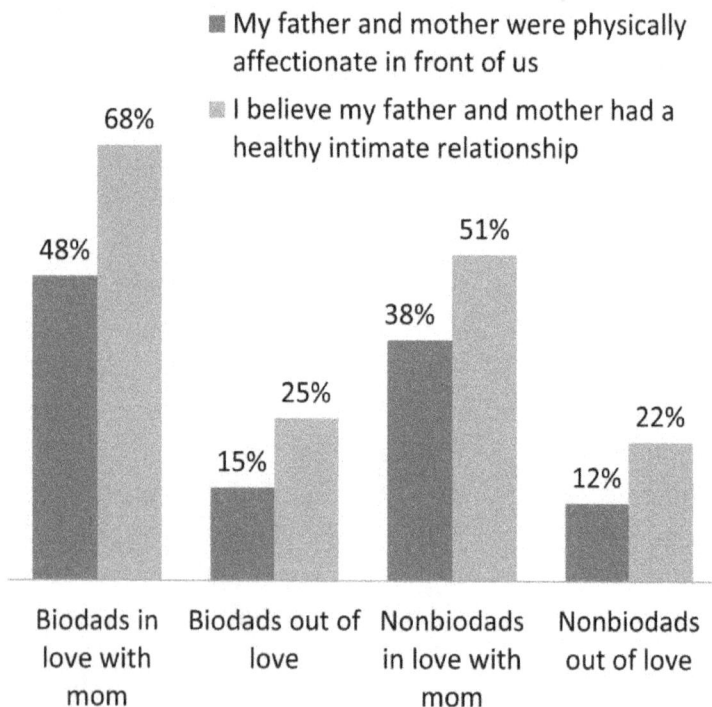

Base: Those raised by married parents at least for some period; n=919
For divorced parents, respondents replied for the pre-divorce period

who loved mom compared to the low of 12% for nonbiodads who didn't love mom (see figure 9).

Perhaps it's some consolation that even if we did not witness a lot of physical affection at home, 44% of us "believe that my father and mother had a healthy intimate relationship." For those of us with biodads that loved mom, the number swells to 68% which basically means that even if we didn't get to see it, we had a hunch that a loving mom and dad had it going on behind closed doors. Good for them.

As for me, I have decided to spare my kids the uncertainty. Much to their chagrin, none of my children could ever honestly report on a survey or anywhere else that their parents don't display affection at home. They'll forgive me some day when their own marriages are as happily affectionate as mine.

Workbook 5:

Answer these questions on a scale from 1 to 10 where 1 = does not describe my father and 10 = describes my father completely:

☐ My father supported my mother

☐ My father thought my mother was beautiful

☐ My father treated my mother with respect

☐ My father and mother were physically affectionate in front of me/us

☐ I believe my father and mother had a healthy intimate relationship

In the prior pages you have the actual responses for each of the four groups we're following in this book. Use the technique I showed you of adding a zero to your scores above so you can compare your answers to everyone else's. How do you fare?

Use this time to think of the moments of support, respect, and attraction you were witness to between your parents. Even if they fought a lot and even if the relationship eventually ended in divorce, there should be plenty of evidence of those things. Consider those moments and experiences. It's likely that you will see foreshadows of your own adult relationships in what you witnessed between your parents. What specific comparisons can you make?

In my case, I have been amazed as my own father's style and words have emerged in my own marriage. That's both good and bad. But my favorite memory of my father in this respect has to be that of my wedding day. We had an early morning wedding and my father and I drove up early to check in before everyone else. It was dark out, the sun had yet to break through and melt the snowfall of the night before, and there wasn't a lot of conversation as we drove north up I-15 to Salt Lake City. I asked him if he had any last advice for me as I embarked on this important adventure and he said he had just one thing to offer.

"Women," he said, "don't think like men."

This was years before Mars and Venus, mind you. The short conversation that ensued has stuck with me ever since. The simplicity of his statement and his sincere hope that I would understand that marrying a woman means signing up to support her, even if you don't always see things the way she does, has proven itself true more times and in more ways than I could have comprehended at the time.

Now it's your turn. What specific lessons did you learn about how to make a marriage last from your father? You can still answer this question even if you learned these lessons by watching your own parents struggle.

_____

_____

_____

_____

_____

_____

6: Dad Taught Us How to Raise the Next Generation

The earliest memories I have of my own father involve, however indirectly, Michael Caine. The actor was the star of the 1966 movie, *Alfie*, which generated the theme song, *What's It All About, Alfie?,* an award-winning song sung by Dionne Warwick. I wouldn't know these facts for many years.

Instead, what I did know was that my father, when he wanted to be silly with us boys, would sing the first line, "What's it all about," and then he would poise his hand over our knees or our bellies or whatever tender part was proximate, and hold out the word "about" while we squirmed, awaiting that moment when he would finally land his attack with an amped-up "Al-fie!" separated into two distinct syllables, each one coinciding with a devastating tickle.

It was one of my favorite parts of being with my dad in my earliest years. That moment of menacing tickle, the anticipation of the strike that was too much to bear yet too unbearable not to hope for, that was the very meaning of childhood bliss to me.

Even growing up I was completely unaware of the original movie. As there were no VCRs, no cable movie channels and certainly no YouTube, it was impossible for me to make the connection. Even when the Jude Law remake came around in 2004 I never bothered to watch the movie or indulge in any nostalgia about the 1966 original. In fact, it was only last year that I finally hit IMDB to look for clips of the original. Even though Michael Caine is an actor's actor, a professional, he is also – at least in my relatively young mind – old. Which is why it was a real shock to see clips of him as a young Don Juan, scandalously seducing women left and right.

Though it's probably something I owe the universe – to watch the whole movie, to see what it is that left such a lasting impression that my father decided to make this his parental theme song. But after viewing the clips and listening to the theme song on YouTube, I have to admit: I prefer the original. And by original I mean the version my father sang.

It's the same version I sang to my own babies as they lay helplessly on the ground, waiting for daddy's claw hand to attack their exposed bellies, practically breathless with anticipation, eager for the moment when I would break the word Alfie into two separate tickle motions. The laughter, the doubling up to prevent further tickle attacks, all of it I passed on from one generation to the next and it worked like clockwork. Always, when the hysteria subsided, there was the same word, repeated twice.

"Again, again."

And with this scene, I pass on, from father to son, a lesson I never intended to learn but proudly share with future generations. It's one of the things that dads do without planning to – they teach us how to take care of the next generation. But in so doing, are we glad for what they taught us or does it make us cringe?

To answer this, let's start with this fact: Only 12% of the people I surveyed said they do not have nor want to have children. And this number only varies slightly by the type of father we had, ranging from a low of 9% to a high of 14%. So despite the supposed decline of the family, nearly 9 in 10 of us want or have children. The effect of fathers is more subtle than that, however, acting in ways that are more fundamental than the desire to have children. Instead, the type of father we have determines how confident we are in raising the next generation.

I gave people the ability to tell me if they have children already and if they think they are or will be good parents. The good news is that the vast majority of us are or want to be parents and also believe that we are or will be good parents. While we might be tempted in our most cynical moments to chalk that up to wishful thinking, remember that for most of us, our fathers were a positive influence from whom we learned many important lessons. The idea that we would imagine ourselves capable of doing the same is not outlandish.

But for those who doubt their ability, the numbers, although small, are admittedly disheartening. If we combine the people who doubt they are or will be good

Figure 10: Some Scared by or Unsure about Parenting

■ Those who are not sure they are or will be good parents

■ Those not sure they are/will be good parents combined with those who don't want to be parents

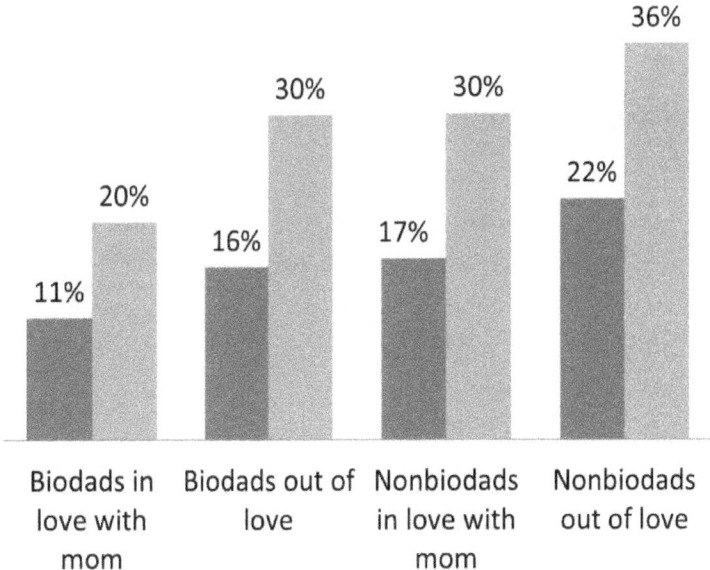

	Biodads in love with mom	Biodads out of love	Nonbiodads in love with mom	Nonbiodads out of love
Not sure	11%	16%	17%	22%
Combined	20%	30%	30%	36%

Base: All respondents; n=1000

parents, regardless of their current status as parents, we find a sad little trend. Just 11% of people raised by biodads in love with mom fall into this category – people who doubt their parenting abilities (see figure 10). But as we move across the quadrants, the numbers rise slowly, to 16% for those raised by biodads not in love with mom, 17% for nonbiodads in love with mom, and 22% for nonbiodads that didn't love mom. The differences are small, though potentially meaningful. They are made even more ominous when we add in those in each group that have already decided that they do not want to have children. Those numbers range from a low of 20% for those raised by biodads in love with mom, to 30% for either those raised by biodads not in love or by non-biodads that loved mom, to a disheartening 36% of those raised by nonbiodads that fell out of love with mom.

The message is clear: Emerging into adulthood confident that you can and will be a good parent is hard enough – 20% of the most advantaged kids don't do it. But when you take away the advantages of a stable and loving home, the number escalates to more than a third of us.

You know enough about my four groups by now that you probably have a good sense of how they are likely to respond to an array of related questions. So I want you to guess their answers to the next question to see how good you are. If I took just those of them that are currently fathers and gave them a list of statements about their feelings of becoming fathers, how do you think they would agree with this statement, "I had a lot to learn about being a father"?

Now the test: Will the men – now fathers themselves – who had the least advantaged father situation be the most concerned or the least concerned about their own father skills? Given what we know about their own dads and their outcomes, shouldn't these men have the most to fear about their own father skill and therefore be the most concerned?

Paradoxically, no. It is the men raised by the better dads who are the most humble in the face of the task. More than half – 55% – of the men raised by biodads that loved mom thought they had a lot to learn. This compares to the low 29% among fathers raised by nonbiodads where love was lacking. That's nearly twice the rate of concern in what might seem to be the wrong direction.

Similarly, the most advantaged dads in my survey were also the most likely to say they were "nervous to be taking on the responsibility of being a father," at 50% compared to 36% among those raised by nonbiodads that didn't love mom.

What's going on here? My best explanation for this is that the men best prepared for fatherhood are also those who are most willing to understand what a daunting and all-in commitment it will be. They are this way, I believe, because they had the better examples in their own lives, examples that they want to live up to. So while – as I said before – they are more likely to want to be fathers and to think they can be good fathers, they are more willing to admit to themselves and to me in my survey that it won't be easy. This type of humility is probably a good thing. It just might be the kind of thinking that prevents the patriarchal abuses some imagine run rampant among fathers.

This is especially likely when we consider the rest of the attitudes and behaviors of the fathers I surveyed. Which fathers thought that the birth of their first child was "a beautiful miracle"? True to form, 68% of those raised by their own biological fathers that loved their mothers said the birth was a miracle, compared to 54% for the two groups in the middle and a low of 42% for those raised by nonbiodads where love was lacking (see figure 11).

Figure 11: Dads Raised by Better Dads See More Beauty

"The birth [of my first child] was a beautiful miracle."

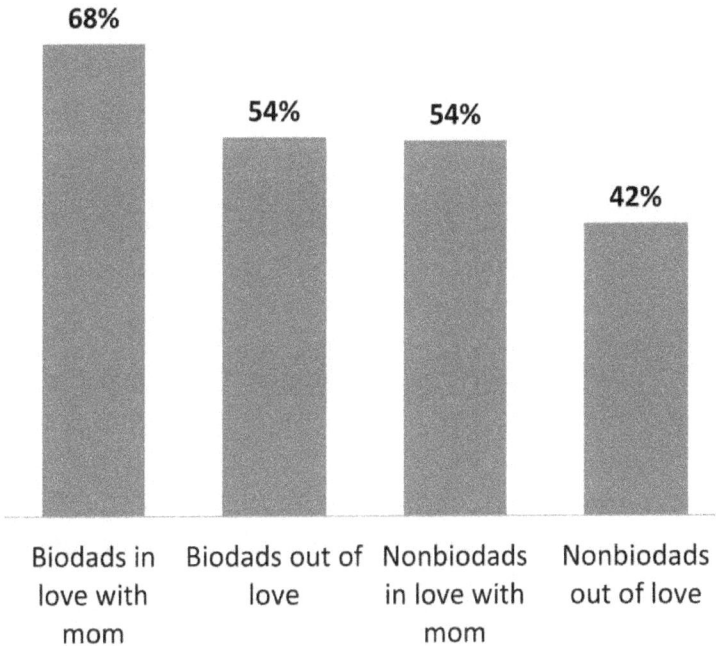

Biodads in love with mom	Biodads out of love	Nonbiodads in love with mom	Nonbiodads out of love

Base: Respondents that are also fathers; n=247

The good news about all of the dads I surveyed is that they were willing to agree that fatherhood is overwhelmingly positive, regardless of their own upbringing. Nearly all – 96% of them – said that "being a father is one of the most important things I have done in my life," a number which varied little by group, ranging from 99% to 94%. Adjectives at the top of the list included rewarding, meaningful, wonderful, and fulfilling, all of which came in above 90% for all groups.

In fact, few of these fathers shied away from overly sentimental assessments of their situations. Nine out of ten of all of these fathers agreed that, "The world would be a better place if more men chose to be good fathers." And nearly the same number said that, "I am a better man because I have been a father." They fall into what some might claim are cliché statements like, "Take advantage of every moment, the kids grow up very fast," a sentiment that more than 90% agree with.

But sadly, though their attitudes are admirable, the kind of father they had carries through to their actual behaviors in unfortunate ways, including their relationships with their own children. Where 92% of those raised by biodads who loved mom say they get along great with their own offspring, the number falls to as low as 77% for those raised by nonbiodads that didn't love mom. Still a good number, to be sure, but the fact that the numbers differ even if they have similarly high hopes for and feelings about fatherhood is discouraging.

And back to the topic of whether or not these fathers are able to show their children how to love a woman, while 82% of the most advantaged group say that "I support my wife and my child(ren) know it," just 59% of the least advantaged group say the same. Worse still, 74% of the advantaged group that are now fathers say that "I treat my wife with respect," compared to 41% of the least advantaged dads who claim the same.

The protective father in me wants to shake these men. "Do not repeat history," I want to say. But how would they have learned how to be good fathers if they had no one to show them?

Workbook 6:

I asked my brother to proofread *Why We Need Dad* in its final stages. This I did for reasons beyond just grammar and syntax. I also wanted to make sure I hadn't misrepresented our family in any way that would come back to haunt me.

This is one chapter that he had to chuckle about because he said, *"Alfie,* for some reason, is in my iTunes library but I don't have a physical memory of it like you do." This could be because my brother was already older when the song came out and was less likely to be the object of an Al-fie attack than I was. Though he didn't have memories of that specific song, he did add, "I just remember Dad singing ALL the time." Which is an interesting memory given that if you asked me which of my parents sang all the time it would certainly be my mother, the opera-trained soprano.

It was precisely these differing memories and reactions that gave me the idea for this workbook version of *Why We Need Dad.* In just the few exchanges I've had with my family about these memories I have uncovered slightly different memories or discovered that different members of the family have drawn different lessons from the same events.

This chapter is one where I would encourage this kind of reflection and discussion and so I did not ask you to answer questions on a scale from one to ten. Because at this point things are getting serious. We can see the long-term effects of having dads that were either better or worse at the job. Plus, it's getting harder for me to construct questions that apply to everyone because, as you see in the analysis, it's now less about your father and more about you.

So what about you? What did you learn about parenting and how have you applied those lessons? If you're not a parent yet, do you want to be? And how did your own experience with your father (and mother) shape your interest in parenting?

Importantly, how do you think you will preserve the best parts of what your father and mother did while improving on their efforts so that in the next generation, when your children drag this book out of the attic and thumb through it, their answers are even better than yours?

_____

_____

_____

_____

_____

7: Why Dad Needs Us to Need Him

Birth really is a bad decision. I wouldn't recommend anybody be born, if they can help it. As the husband of a woman who has chosen to be on the receiving end of birth six times, I remain in complete and utter awe of the whole thing. Birth is possibly the most animal thing we do which makes it sound natural and wonderful and all that – and it certainly is, but only hours and even days after it's over can you honestly talk about it like that. Just before, during, and immediately after, birth is simply a really bad idea.

Our first birth took some incredible number of hours, my wife counts it at over 30. The first trip to the hospital was the one I was the least prepared for. Yes, we had our little case packed, we knew where we were supposed to go, and we had carefully timed the contractions. But no, having a case and a plan and a watch don't equal having a clue, something the hospital confirmed almost immediately when they observed, measured, examined, and reported that, sure enough, we were, as most first-time parents are, completely stupid and should never have come to the hospital in the first place. I next expected them to say that God had called, admitted he had made a mistake in trusting the two of us to have a child and that he was going to take this one back. After all, we couldn't even be trusted to go to the hospital at the right time.

It was the next day before we finally went back having documented hours upon hours of contractions so we could make the case to the hospital judge that we deserved to be convicted of imminent parenthood. I also tried to hold us out as long as possible – there was some twisted part of me that wanted my wife to be in such tremendous, howling pain before we returned so that we could present ourselves as the couple tragically martyred by the hospital's prior rejection of them.

This does happen all the time, of course. One of my favorite stories from a friend was the time they went to the hospital in a huge Nor'easter (that's the kind of New England storm that produced the book and movie *The Perfect Storm*) to notify the hospital that they were ready to deliver their fourth child any minute now. The hospital tsk-tsked them and sent them home, patting them on their little heads and explaining that a mother of three, soon to be four children doesn't know when her own body is ready to deliver, the nice, big hospital does.

Shortly thereafter their daughter was born in the car on the side of the road in a torrential downpour, delivered by her dad who helped pull her out with one hand while he put the car in park with the other.

They named her Carly.

At least Carly's dad got to be a superstar. I have rehearsed in my mind all the ways I could deliver my own child if the need arose and then I have nearly wet myself each time we've gone into labor, imagining what would happen if I didn't get my wife to the doctor or midwives in time.

Perhaps because the Good Lord knows not to put me in that situation, I have never been forced to deliver my child with one or even two hands, in a downpour or a dryspell. Instead, I'm the guy who parks the car, checks in at the hospital, and carries the bag. That's right, the manliest thing I have ever done in the delivery of my children is carry an oversized purse.

I'm convinced that this is why men are supposed to bring a camera to the delivery. It gives them something manly to do – play with gadgets. "Look, honey! When I shift the camera to sepia mode you can't even see how red the blood...is..." at which point the manly man with the manly device keels over. The delivery staff just brushes him to one side like so much afterbirth and continues on with their work.

I can at least say I have remained conscious during all six deliveries.

Which I'm glad about because I have loved every single one of them. There I am, in my roller coaster car, buckled in tight, racing up and down, making hairpin turns, terrified each time we lose the baby's heartbeat and thrilled each time it comes back, absolutely mortified when I watch the love of my life descend into the valley of the shadow of death and then delirious when she revives enough to make a joke.

My favorite joke of hers during the rather prolonged birth of baby number six: "Did anybody bring a pocketknife? Let's just cut this baby out!" Ha, ha. Ha.

When it's all over, when the baby emerges and you see a quasi-human form present itself to you for the first time, when the volume of mass and fluid in your wife's abdomen reduces by ten or more pounds in a single stroke, that's when the magic comes.

Even now, sitting at my keyboard twenty years from the first time and five years from the sixth, I can summon those moments with brilliant clarity. I recall the admixture of wonder, fatigue, and bliss that overcame me each time. I know enough about neurochemistry and hormones to know that it's a ploy on nature's part to make me love my child so I will provide for it. And I know that the feeling of admiration and awe that overwhelms me when I look at my exhausted wife is a similar chemical manipulation of my senses to make me loyal to her for life.

I don't care. Bring on the hormones. In fact, maybe more of us need more of those hormones. Not just for the benefit of the next generation, but for our own wellbeing. I have argued here that we need dad and even though I have just skimmed the surface of the data I collected, I hope it's clear that we do need dad.

But what about the effect of being the dad? I already shared the feelings that my respondents who are themselves fathers have about it. It's superlative, they wouldn't trade it for the world. But that's not reason enough to make it social policy that more men earnestly prepare themselves for and accept the responsibility of becoming a good father, is it?

If your answer is still not yes, consider this last analysis of my data: It turns out that being a good father makes dad's life better long after fatherhood.

I only included a few questions here, mostly as an afterthought, because it wasn't my intent to measure the life outcomes of the fathers themselves. But upon analysis of the results, I'm glad I asked. For example, consider the current health of your father (if still alive). Two thirds (67%) of biodads who loved mom are currently healthy (see figure 12). Coming in second are the 59% of nonbiodads who loved mom. If the love was lacking, health outcomes fall precipitously: 38% of biodads that didn't love mom and just 31% of

nonbiodads that didn't love mom are currently healthy.
That's half the health rate of the top group.

Figure 12: Dads That Raised Us Well Fare Better

"Which of the following statements about your father are
true today?"   ■ He is currently healthy

■ I speak to him on the phone often

■ He is happy

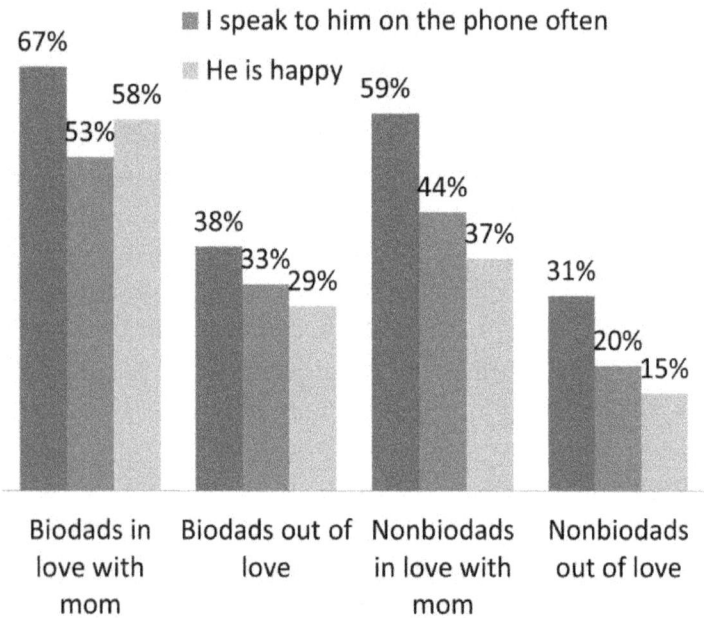

	Biodads in love with mom	Biodads out of love	Nonbiodads in love with mom	Nonbiodads out of love
He is currently healthy	67%	38%	59%	31%
I speak to him on the phone often	53%	33%	44%	20%
He is happy	58%	29%	37%	15%

Base: Respondents whose fathers are still alive today; n=655

I know enough about science and statistics to know that
being a good dad didn't cause these health benefits. But
it is clear that being a good dad – especially one who
knows how to love a woman – correlates with long-term
health benefits. It's entirely possible that a man who

doesn't know how to raise children well or love a woman with all his heart also falls into health patterns that are destructive. But it's also likely that a man who can't sustain the most important relationships in his life is a man who will experience and possibly succumb to sorrow and the malaise such sorrow can conjure.

It's not just individual outcomes that differ, however. Something as basic as human contact, the very contact we probably need to avoid negative long-term health outcomes, is dictated by what kinds of father-child relationships men managed. While 53% of those raised by a biodad that loved mom say that they "speak to him on the phone often," the same can only be said of 20% of those raised by a nonbiodad that didn't love mom. In-person visits don't fall far behind – 47% of the most advantaged children say they visit dad in-person often compared to 17% among the least advantaged.

And then there's the matter of happiness. Happiness studies have been all the rage as of late and many consistent variables point to increased happiness such as religious conviction and marriage. But based on my initial survey, for fathers whose children are grown to adulthood, the type of father they were is a significant predictor of the happiness their children estimate they are experiencing today if still alive. A meaningful 58% of those biodads that loved mom are happy, according to their kids' estimates. The children of just 15% of the nonbiodads that didn't love mom can say the same about them.

Kind of makes you want to go call, visit, and hug dad, doesn't it?

Workbook 7:

Answer these questions on a scale from 1 to 10 where 1 = does not describe my father and 10 = describes my father completely. If your father is no longer living, you can answer reflecting on his last years:

☐ My father is currently healthy

☐ I speak to my father often

☐ I visit my father in person often

☐ My father is happy

Here again, you add a zero to your answers and then thumb back to page 94 to see how your father fares compared to fathers generally. One likely outcome of reading this chapter and answering these questions is that your father is probably going to get a phone call if he's still alive. If he's not, I imagine there might be an extra flower on his grave soon.

It's certainly what happened to me when writing this book. I know that my job as a son is to raise my children to be a gift to my parents. So I typically keep my head down and do my job without calling them to say hi that often. I usually think that my parents are content with that, at least as long as their grandchildren turn out okay. But halfway through this book I called my parents to let them know that their granddaughter was going to run the Boston Marathon and invited them to come visit for that week, which happens to coincide with their birthdays. Maybe I was compensating just a little.

I won't make you jealous with everything we did with them while they were here but the short list includes club-level tickets to opening day at Fenway Park and an evening at Ming Tsai's signature restaurant in Wellesley. Wish you could have been there.

Along the way, I took stock. My parents – both my father and mother in my case – have taken good care of me. Have I made sure they know that I am prepared to take care of them? I'm sure there's a whole survey yet to conduct about taking care of your father as he prepares for his last days, months or years of life, but I didn't want to wait for that moment to come before I contemplated my father's wellbeing.

In a story that is too important to include as an afterthought but will certainly make it into *Finding Fathers*, the sequel to this book, I learned from my own father the importance of acting on those small promptings, those feelings that whisper that you should cherish your father before it's too late. Your homework for this chapter? Do that.

8: A Word in Closing

It's my own fault. I'm the one who titled this book *Why We Need Dad* but that's not really what this book is about, which I can see clearly now. It's true that I've shared what I hope are compelling data about the role of fathers. And I do believe that that data show very clearly that fathers are important in ways that it is no longer fashionable to admit. I showed how our dads were men of character. I showed how hard they worked for us and how positive the influence of dad as a provider was for us. I demonstrated the ways that dads teach us how to make marriage work and how to raise the next generation. I also showed – in an almost painfully clear way – how dad really needs us to need him, for his own benefit.

But only now, after spending the money and the time to pull all this together do I realize that if my goal is to prevent us from excising dad from our lives like an unnecessary appendage, it may be too late. The operation is underway and for many of us, irreversible incisions have already been made. Certainly the tide of social opinion – at least as the media would have us read it – has already concluded that dads are a hassle if not downright impossible. Whether the media have led us there or whether they are just reflecting our own wishes, it is true that all the trends point away from dad. Even though my data show clearly just how valuable fathers are and how happy most of us are with our dads, my data also show that many are gradually weaning themselves away from the benefits of having or being a father. And every indicator of long-term wellbeing I measured points downward because of it, from the inability of some to perceive the miracle of their own child's birth to the feeling of new, unprepared fathers that they aren't getting the love they need in their relationships.

As evidence, consider the men in my survey who are married and have chosen to become fathers. An overwhelming 86% of them report that they are very in love with their wives. Happily, even in the group with the least advantaged upbringing – those raised by a nonbiodad who did not love mom – 71% can say the same, a smaller number to be sure, but a high number. Then this: 73% of all the dads in my sample say that, "I think my wife is beautiful and my child(ren) know it." Yet for those raised without a biological dad that loved their mother, the number drops below half to 47%.

Similarly troubling, when we turn it around and ask my respondents who are fathers what they're getting in return for their efforts as fathers, 64% of them say they that they, "Get the love I need from my wife." That's well and good, but here's where being raised by your biological father really counts because for those raised by biodads in love with mom and even those raised by biodads where love ran out the numbers come in at 82% and 72%, respectively. Compare that to a dismal 29% for today's fathers who were raised by any kind of nonbiological father. The point is this: Each failure of one generation gets amplified in the next, growing a wider and wider gap between what we'll need from our next generation of fathers and what they'll be able to give us.

If I started by trying to measure why we need dad, I have ended by finding that if we are seriously pondering dad's relevance as a society, no amount of data I pay to collect can change us from that self-destructive course. Because it shouldn't really take a national survey to determine that dads are not just an appendix in our collective organism, they are more like a chamber of the heart. And without that chamber functioning, I fear that there is no heart-lung machine capable of pumping life-giving love, character, and commitment through the whole social body, not the way dad does. Or did.

Which is why I now understand that my survey doesn't explain why we need dad as much as it foreshadows what life without dad will be like. By tracking the differences between groups that have biological dads that loved mom and those that had exactly the opposite, I can conclude that as dads dwindle, there will be less love, fewer committed relationships, a less stable environment for the next generation to grow up in, and a less potent binding force to keep my own sons' cohort focused on raising that next generation rather than idly playing videogames and surfing internet porn.

This book that was at first glance a nice tribute to fathers has suddenly turned into a pro-father manifesto. I hope that for most of you reading this, you are not angry with me. I'm telling you things you want to hear and are glad to learn. Hopefully you are grateful that someone would take the time to measure and report on the facts about fatherhood, especially when we are otherwise swimming in a world of images and messages that downplay the importance of fathers or shrug off their decline.

But some of you are angry right now for a range of reasons, this one I can at least guess at: If your father was not the noble and good man mine was, it has probably left you feeling cold to hear just how well-off the rest of us are and how harmed we will all be if we don't bring better dads back into vogue. I can sympathize with that perspective even though it isn't my own and I am sorry for your experience. You deserved better.

But I believe this is one truth that can set you free: Your father's shortcomings are not your fault. They don't even have to be his fault for you to take solace in the notion that you are free to surpass them. You are not condemned to live out all the statistical probabilities suggested by my analysis. Instead, rather than see despair in the fathers I have illuminated, you can choose to see hope in these numbers: There are good fathers out there and you can choose to become one or to seek one as your mate – or seek to support your mate as he becomes one. I sincerely hope you do.

And now to another group that might be angry. I am sorry if anything I have said has triggered in you the belief that by elevating fathers I have denigrated or reduced the role of women generally or mothers specifically. I have not said anything to that effect. In fact, I mean quite the opposite with my analysis. None of these lessons we learn from fathers can be learned in their fullest measure without the powerful presence of mothers. In fact, my data clearly support the idea that good fathers are not just critical to solid marriages and families, they are, in fact, made by them.

We have no record of when Nathaniel McQuivey – my fourth great-grandfather – came to Vermont until he was married to Sarah Hall in Pittsford, Vermont, in January of 1802 at approximately 27 years of age. By December of that year, the newlyweds had relocated to the bustling town of Williston, adjacent to what would soon become Burlington. We know this because they had their first child, Harvey, there. He died within the month. Their only child to survive into adulthood, Clara, was born a year later. Their final child, Sally, came in 1807 and it is likely that her arrival is what took Grandma Sarah from this earth shortly thereafter.

I have been to Grandma Sarah's grave. It is the oldest grave of my relatives that I have personally visited. I say relative but she is not actually related to me. But as a first – and may I presume, courageous – wife of my Granddad McQuivey, I love her.

I have sat by her grave marker, I may be the only descendant of Nathaniel McQuivey alive who has done so. It is a ghostly white yet wonderfully warm, soft stone. I have cleared away the lichen and moss and pondered, wondering where the graves of her Harvey and later her Sally – who died three years after her mother – were placed. Were they buried somewhere here, unmarked? Or did they not have the money for a proper burial? I begin to wonder outlandish things far outside of the facts I can confirm, such as did my Granddad McQuivey's in-laws blame him for taking their daughter into the cold and as-of-yet undeveloped North only to bury her there and leave her children without markers?

The whole scene conjures up a dark period in my direct ancestor's life. He had struck forth into the wilderness, walked down his very own road, to carve out a place for himself and his family, relying neither on family land nor political connections. He was a McQuivey, after all, a commoner, a descendant of a Scottish rebel. He had to create his own destiny because he none to inherit.

And for his efforts, he was repaid with the loss of his wife and all but one of their children. As I stood in the cemetery next to Grandma Sarah's headstone, I asked myself what went through his mind then. Whether he considered giving up or not, I don't know. While I can't say for sure what he *felt*, I can attest to what he *did.* Just over a year after putting his beloved Sarah in the ground, he once again chose marriage and fatherhood. And because he did, not only am I here, but I am well. Raised well, loved well, and taught well.

That's why when I reflect on what I have gained from my actual father I am compelled to look beyond him to his father, and his father before him, even farther back, to a line of fathers that are the very embodiment of American fatherhood. From Scottish indentured servant to Ph.D. technology consultant, we McQuiveys have done the same thing over and over: We have struck out to find a place that we can call our own and then have given our children the chance to do the same. It's a squarely American tale, one that has been replicated by Jews,

Mexicans, Pakistanis, and people of many origins harder to trace than mine. It is a story so completely mine, yet so completely universal, that I could not complete my analysis of American fatherhood without acknowledging this universal connection between all of our fathers.

The next chapter in this story of fathers will be written by my boys, each of whom I hope will one day become fathers. And the next chapter by their sons, and so on, for centuries to come. But this chapter, the one I'm completing now, beyond its social implications, is an homage to a man who, on that night so many years ago, made a tough but ultimately correct call. He cancelled the camping trip and surrendered my appendix to the proper authorities and because of that I am still alive. Thus I can reflect on and be grateful for that and other things. I am grateful that I didn't break my back jumping off that cliff, and that once the basketall seasons I agreed to play were over my dad let me quit basketball forever. He continues to teach me what it means to be a father and how hard I should work to imitate him. It is my hope that on this and every Father's Day my father stops to reflect on all that he has done and is proud. I willingly count myself among the 26% of us who said that one thing we would like to accomplish with our fathers in the years we have left is to make our dads proud of us – in my case, prouder than he already deserves to be.

Thank you, Dad.

Book Discussion Group Resources

An Interview with the Author

Q: You admit that you have an "advantaged" father situation. How does that qualify you to write this book?

A: It doesn't. Except that it has plagued me for many years – this idea that I have a wonderful life yet feel I should apologize for it. My parents were good to me and to each other. They are still married after fifty years and they deserve almost all the credit for the fact that their sons are happily married fathers who can provide for their families. Yet I somehow have the impression that I can't speak about fatherhood openly because, well, fatherhood has worked for me so splendidly.

Q: But not everybody has the same advantages that you do. Do you understand how that seems unfair to some?

A: This could be unfair in some people's eyes, I understand that – boastful, even. But I also think it's wrong that people like my father, my parents, people who have managed to pull off something as remarkable as living a good, honorable life, should have children who tiptoe around that fact as if it was somehow wrong to point out what good people they are. America used to be a place where people were held up as paragons of community virtue if they could come from nowhere and turn themselves into something. This was true for Abraham Lincoln and should be true today but it's largely not, not as long as those of us who are the fruits of such industrious living feel embarrassed or intimidated to keep our mouths closed about how we got where we are today.

Q: So you're okay if what you're writing appears insensitive to some.

A: I guess I'm not okay with that, truth be told, because what I'm writing is very important and if people dismiss it because they perceive that I just don't understand what it's like to be them, well, then I will have failed to get my point across. In fact, the people I most want to reach are the people who are at risk for failing the next generation. For all the reasons I've written and many more fatherhood is a net positive, even when people don't do it perfectly it appears to generate much more good than harm. But we don't see that side of it because we spend so much time hearing about the few fathers that failed us.

Q: That's part of your point, isn't it. You undertook this survey precisely because you didn't know how many good fathers there were out there.

A: Exactly. I launched this survey completely blind. I had no idea how many of the people I surveyed would report that they had good fathers and how many would report that they had bad fathers. I have an entire section in the survey about physical abuse because I grew up hearing so much about how abusive fathers are – and as a kid I had friends with fathers I would consider abusive – that I expected to dive into that data in great detail. But the fact is only 35% of the people I surveyed said their fathers ever spanked them or administered any type of corporal punishment. Of those people who were spanked, 53% said that their fathers were "always in control" when they administered their punishment. A similar number said they thought their fathers spanked them to teach them important lessons. In the end, there just wasn't much to say about these abusive fathers because the vast majority of us weren't raised by abusive fathers at all. So it's fair to say I went into this survey expecting dads to be worse than they really are and was quite impressed to find that they had done right by most of us.

Q: That's interesting data, it even supports the idea that fathers aren't as bad as we sometimes think, yet you didn't put that in the book, why not?

A: When it became clear that this book is really about what we learn from our fathers I realized that going down the spanking path might be therapeutic in a different book but not necessarily relevant to this one, I opted to leave it out. It will reappear, however, in a later book, due out within the year. That book, called *Finding Fathers*, is a much more elaborate story and uses the same survey but goes much further into many more topics related to fatherhood.

Q: There's more to say, then?

A: Much more to say, and many more personal things to say about it. This book briefly touches on my own satisfaction with being a father of six remarkable children, but it doesn't even begin to describe the wondrous agony of fatherhood. That's what I hope to capture in the next book, and for that I will have to dive deeper into what it means to be a father, into examples of fathers in literature and film, into the rich heritage I have in my own patriarchal line. There is much, much more to say!

Book Discussion Group Questions

How did your own father experience shape the way you reacted to this book?

Is this a book you would want your own father to read? If so, why, and if not, why not?

The author points out at the end that he does not intend to make mothers seem less important than fathers. Did you feel that his focus failed to give motherhood its due?

What notable fathers stand out to you in literature, TV, or film? Do you find it easier to think of negative or positive examples of fathers in the media?

Is there a father in the media that you wish you could have been raised by, even meaning no disrespect to your own father?

Are you personally concerned about the rising rate of births to unwed mothers or do you think the people who worry about it are being too alarmist?

If you are concerned about any impact of unwed motherhood, what do you think could be done to address the problem?

To partly explain his interest in spending his own money to do this survey, the author wrote the following: "It's true that divorce and fatherlessness are facts of life today. But they are still *choices* and as choices, it is important to point out that we have the ability – and perhaps the obligation – to at least consider if not encourage other choices."

Given that we can't choose who our fathers are or how they act, how valid is his statement about choices we can make with respect to fatherhood?

If someone were to give you money to conduct a study on fatherhood, what questions would you want to ask and why?

If someone were to give you money to conduct a study on a completely different topic, what would it be?

—

If you have questions of your own you'd like to submit, visit facebook.com/WhyWeNeedDad and share your questions and thoughts with other readers.

About the Author

James McQuivey is a media technology analyst at Forrester Research, Inc. where he covers the technologies that have improved and/or disrupted our lives and our businesses. In his career there he has supervised surveys that have totaled over a million respondents. He is occasionally sought out by publications like *The New York Times* and the *Wall Street Journal* for comment on industry events and every once in a while his friends hear him on NPR and wonder if someone else out there is named James McQuivey. But his work there has nothing to do with fatherhood, social policy, or family life in America.

However, his personal life has everything to do with fatherhood and family life in America, if not social policy. As the father of six children – five boys and one girl – he has spent many a restless night fretting over, arguing with, and praying for his children, hoping desperately to be as good a father and parent as his father and mother were and still are.

His primary source of hope for accomplishing this is his marriage to Megan Kelly McQuivey, a mother whom he credits with teaching him the basics of parenting so that he could eventually distinguish himself as a father. They live in the Boston metropolitan area with their four youngest children.

James earned his Ph.D. from Syracuse University's S.I. Newhouse School of Public Communications. Go Orange.

For more information and recent updates on the author, please visit facebook.com/WhyWeNeedDad.

Appendix A - Methodology

All the survey data presented in *Why We Need Dad* come from the Finding Fathers Study, a private survey designed and paid for by James McQuivey. The research firm Research Now fielded the survey from December 15th through December 29th, 2011, providing the online sample, representative of US adults from 18- to 75-years old. A total of 1,126 began the survey but 126 were screened out because they indicated there was no person in their lives that they considered a father figure, leaving a final n of 1,000. The outbound sample was balanced to be even on gender and representative on major age categories. No other outbound sampling was done and the data were not weighted to any predefined parameters.

Excerpt from *Finding Fathers*

From the next work on fatherhood by James McQuivey, expected within the year:

The water is trying to kill me. This is the first semi-rational thought I have had in several hours, and if this is the best I can do, it is not a good sign. It's 2am, I survey my situation: I have two plastic, wide-mouthed water pitchers in hand and with them I am scooping – left hand, right hand, left hand right hand – through the Sea of McQuivey, formerly known as my basement. With these pitchers I collect icy water and pour it into a plastic storage bin in which sits an evil looking device that gurgles and sucks the water, ultimately pumping it up an old garden hose and away from my basement. I have been doing this continuously for four hours and I am tired and maybe just a bit paranoid. Knowing this, I should think twice before saying so, but I repeat: the water is trying to kill me.

It is Tuesday, March 16th, 2010 and in four hours it will be a full 24 hours since the foundation of my home started heaving upward under the influence of something called hydrostatic pressure. Let me spare you the engineering details, but suffice it to say that if the water pressure under your home rises to a level that exceeds the weight of the concrete floor of your basement, it will gently lift skyward, just enough for those thousands of pounds of water pressure to force life-giving H2O in between your cement floor and the cement footing on which the floor rests.

The result? Water. Not just leaking, or seeping, but eventually running through your home in streams that soon become rivers that soon become a lake that will rise as high as it needs to to balance the rising level of the water table outside.

I didn't know that this was possible. This home, the one I have just spent all of my credit to remodel, now literally appears to be coming apart at the seams. It has been raining for three days straight such that the ground outside is like a massive, sopped sponge. And just a few short days ago, as several friends and neighbors with leaky New England basements reported their own diluvial adventures, I had congratulated myself that my concrete foundation walls remained without blemish.

But of hydrostatic pressure I knew naught. Until Monday morning. First there was the maddening rush to get everything up off the floor, especially out of my office where decades of photos and home videos rest on the floor in soon-to-be-soggy cardboard boxes. There was the scramble to find a pump, any pump, once we realized that 28 towels and a wet-dry vac were no match for a rising water table. And there was the stream of wonderful friends who came to help carry waterlogged boxes upstairs and to lift furniture up and out of the way while we scrambled to find the only pumps in the Boston metro area that someone smarter than us hadn't already bought.

I spent most of the day ankle deep in water, calculating how many pumps we had (answer: three, including the one a friend drove to New Hampshire to buy) and how continuously we would need to work to keep the water from rising above the six inch level, thus keeping it away from our electrical system, boiler, oil tank, and appliances. By nightfall, I found that two pumps running solid could not keep the water level from rising. Which you might assume is fine, because I already told you we had three pumps. But one of the pumps isn't exactly designed for this setup. It is a sump pump designed to operate in pits filled with at least eight inches of water. If I waited for the water level to reach eight inches, I'd have to shut down the electricity in the basement as well as the boiler. In other words, we'd have to move out.

And by "we," I mean myself, my wife, Megan, and our six children. Moving out was the option I was not willing to consider (despite many wonderful friends who offered). I say all of this by way of explanation. Else, why would I be up at 2am, scooping up water with pitchers and tossing it into a 16-inch deep Rubbermaid storage bin where pump number three could suck it up and thereby aid the other two pumps in the process of keeping us from moving out of our home?

My feet are freezing. I have been wearing Crocs all day because they do not get soggy in water. But, if you are familiar with the fashion faux pas known as Crocs, you also know that they are full of holes. As such, my feet have been lovingly bathed in frigid groundwater for most of the day. I haven't eaten much and I'm confident my cortisol levels are far recommended levels.

But instead of in bed, asleep, releasing growth hormone and countering the effects of stress, I am feeling sorry for myself in my basement, cold and alone. That's when it hits me, originating in a deep, suspicious part of my brain: The water is trying to kill me.

Trust me on this, that part of me says. How could you not see the pattern? Remember Hawaii? Remember Lake Powell? Remember [that lake in New Hampshire I won't disclose because I don't want you to go there and spoil it]? You'd have to be a fool not to realize that this is a conspiracy. Water has your number. It's trying to kill you and it has been from the moment you left its most benign counterpart – the amniotic fluid of your birth.

Of course, I say to myself, you are so right. Water is trying to kill me.

Yesss, it hisses, as all tempting but wrong thoughts seem to do. And if it can't kill you, it will settle for your family.

I am many things, I am a man, a writer, an analyst, a market researcher, a graduate of this school, a former fellow at that one, briefly a professor at yet another one, and thanks to some tremendous patience on the part of my doctoral advisor, I am a certified Ph.D. But of all the titles that apply to me, there are two that matter most: husband, father.

I am grateful that the two titles I care about most are inextricably intertwined. In my case, I am not one without the other, though I know many people have managed to unwind their own connections between the two (or avoid twisting them up in the first place). For myself, I am happily, deliriously both of these things.

And as I sit in the basement, feet turning a deeper shade of blue than I knew was possible, it is that identity that drives me nearly out of my mind.

Because this is my home. No matter how evolved man has become in the post-feminist era, there is a part of me that roars to life when I contemplate my cave, my castle, my home in danger. The actual edifice is a pain, it requires too much upkeep, it has recently put us through that special type of marriage crisis called "remodeling," and it is far from anyone's idea of a dream home. But in the end, my home is my shelter, and the only reason I bother with any of it is so that I may extend that shelter – in a throwback, caveman-like way – to my dear wife and our six children.

And now the rising water wants to take that all away from me, literally eroding the foundation of my home, mocking my protective ability and pressing, hour after hour, against whatever pride I have left.

I know – later, upon reflection – that this is silly. But at 2am, when I'm desperately eager to sleep for an hour but don't want to rob my wife of the sleep that she deserves, I talk myself in circles on this topic and I am convinced that my entire role as husband and father is now tied to my ability to recover from this disaster, to drive the demon-water from my home thus fortifying my castle against future invasion.

I consider that thought for a moment, and I genuinely try to rally. But I fail. Within a few minutes, after bailing furiously to get the water level down a quarter inch, I use the time I just bought to drag myself upstairs and ask Megan if she'll take a turn bailing while I sleep.

This is a book about fatherhood, something you might have suspected by the title *Finding Fathers*. It's a book that has been hatching inside of me for years, starting with the moment Brian, my father-in-law, walked out his front door – with me towing my days-old baby boy in a fancy, padded car seat – and with a big smile on his face, asked, "Now you see what it's all about?"

A writer himself, he's got a spare, Hemingway style. His question was simple and pointed. I got its full meaning right away. A similarly big smile came over my face and I nodded.

"Yes, I do see what it's all about."

I did see, at the time. That fatherhood was the summum bonum of a man's life, that it was the highest elevation that we could seek, that we could struggle all the days of our lives and never accomplish anything more grand than a well-loved and well-raised child.

But what I have come to see in the twenty years since then is that he may have also meant something more complex than that – that fatherhood would soon become my master, my all-consuming thought, the thing that brought me to the lowest lows punctuated by brief and exhilarating highs, that, in fact, my life would be "all about" doing my duty by my children. Whether he meant that or not, I see it now, too.

The experience of fatherhood is simultaneously individual and universal. In these pages you will find things that you can immediately relate to, whether you are a father or the product of one. But the universals I will share with you have come to me through such individual experiences – like wrestling a three-year old to zip up his coat in the snow while my own father watches, a restrained patience showing on his face – that it's impossible to imagine sharing them with you in any way that could be meaningful en masse, without us sitting down, one on one, and chatting over a cup of cocoa.

So I have cheated. In this book I will tell my story of fatherhood, of my search for it. But I will also link it to yours, figuratively speaking, because I have surveyed one thousand people about fatherhood. In and among the 1,000 I have included several hundred fathers. And I have had them all help me search for the universals of fatherhood. Whether it's finding out that 48% of our fathers have ever asked us if we are "trying to cool/heat the whole outside?" by leaving the door open or by learning that 21% of fathers have experienced the unfathomable pain of entrusting a child to the icy arms of death. That way, the stories that I will tell are not just my own, they are the stories of all of us.

I do not write this book because there is a new crisis of fatherhood coming. There has always been and will always continue to be a crisis of fatherhood. Instead, I write this book because my own experience of fatherhood has been one of continual crisis and renewal. I hope that by sharing my journey to find my own fatherhood, I might help you on your own journey, whether to be a better father or to connect more fully to your very own.

Of course, whether you encourage everyone you know to buy this book as a great Father's Day gift is entirely up to you. No pressure. Really.

—

Thank you for your interest in *Finding Fathers*. To be notified when the book is released, please visit Why We Need Dad at facebook.com/WhyWeNeedDad